Other Books by Lupa

Fang and Fur, Blood and Bone: A Primal Guide to Animal Magic (Megalithica Books, 2006)

A Field Guide to Otherkin (Megalithica Books, 2007)

DIY Totemism: Your Personal Guide to Animal Totems (Megalithica Books, 2008)

Engaging the Spirit World: Shamanism, Totemism, and Other Animistic Practices (Immanion Press, 2009)

Skin Spirits: The Spiritual and Magical Use of Animal Parts (Megalithica Books, 2010)

New Paths to Animal Totems

About the Author

Lupa is a neoshaman, artist, and sustainability geek living in Portland, OR. She has been working with animal magic in various forms since the mid-1990s. While her path has wended through various experiences over the years, she has spent her most recent time developing therioshamanism, a self-created and spirit-directed neoshamanic path. She possesses a master's degree in counseling psychology with an emphasis on ecopsychology, and integrates elements of this education into her practice and writing. Additionally, she has several publications on animal magic and related topics under her belt that may be found all over the Internet. When she isn't breaking keyboards with her furious typing, Lupa is most likely hiding in the Columbia River Gorge making ritual tools and other art out of hides, bones, and other such things, as well as finding ways to make her apartment greener without making the rental company look askance. She may be found online at http://www.thegreenwolf.com and http://therioshamamism.com. You can email her at lupa.greenwolf@gmail.com.

New Paths to Animal Totems

Three Alternative Approaches to Creating Your Own Totemism

Lupa

Llewellyn Worldwide
Woodbury, Minnesota

FIRST EDITION
First Printing, 2012

Book design by Bob Gaul
Cover design by Kevin R. Brown
Cover art: Dolphin © iStockphoto.com/tirc83
    Bobcat © iStockphoto.com/Images in the Wild
    Blue jay © iStockphoto.com/breckeni
    Owl © iStockphoto.com/Holly Kuchera
    Giraffe © iStockphoto.com/Peter Malsbury
    Fox © iStockphoto.com/Paul Binet
Editing by Laura Graves

Llewellyn Publications is a registered trademark of Llewellyn Worldwide Ltd.

Library of Congress Cataloging-in-Publication Data
Lupa.
  New paths to animal totemism/Lupa.—1st ed.
    p. cm.
  Includes bibliographical references and index.
  ISBN 978-0-7387-3337-1
1. Animals—Miscellanea. 2. Totems—Miscellanea. I. Title.
  BF1623.A55L87 2012
  133'.259—dc23
                    2012028940

Llewellyn Publications
A Division of Llewellyn Worldwide Ltd.
2143 Wooddale Drive
Woodbury, MN 55125-2989
www.llewellyn.com

Printed in the United States of America

To my parents, for encouraging me with books even in the crib (and for patiently taping the books back together again and again and again...) and for sitting with me all those elementary school nights going over each sentence of my writing in detail. Yours is the garden from which my love of reading and writing took root.

And to S., for believing in me and supporting me even when I couldn't give those things to myself, and for your deep wells of creativity and inspiration. Yours truly.

Acknowledgments

To Taylor Ellwood, for helping me get my professional writing career going and reminding me to never stop trying new things. To Elysia Gallo, for encouraging me to write this book in the first place, and for patiently answering the barrage of questions through the initial edits. To Laura Graves, for further polishing up the rough edges of this work and being most excellent to work with.

Most of all, to all the readers, fans, friends, acquaintances, and other wonderfully supportive people who have bought the books, read the ideas, teased them out into new forms, and reminded me why I write in the first place. I hope you love this one.

Contents

A Note to Readers

I've always been fascinated by animals. Even when I was a toddler first acquainting myself with the wide green world of my backyard, one of my first discoveries was the existence of roly-polies (also less adorably known as "pill bugs"). Later on, I learned about everything from grasshoppers to garter snakes—often through catching them and keeping them for temporary observation on the back porch. I was also that kid that the neighbors called in for pet sitting, since I was often in their yard playing with the dogs and cats anyway. And, of course, there were the various furry, feathered, and finned critters in my own home over the years.

So it was no surprise that when I was introduced to Pagan spiritualities and magic in the mid-1990s, one of the first things I gravitated toward was animal totemism. (If you'll forgive the pun, it was a natural fit!) Like so many other people, my first book on the subject was Ted Andrews's *Animal-Speak*. After reading Andrews's interpretations of dozens of totems and seeing the exercises he promoted as ways to connect more deeply with them, I was pretty impressed. However, being the independent person I am, I decided to make my own relationships with the totems on my own terms.

In the decade and change since then, I have created a variety of methods for working with the totems. Some of these were based in generic Wicca-flavored Neopaganism. I also spent a few years primarily working with chaos magic, which gave my totemism and animal magic a much more do-it-yourself feel. For the past several years, I've settled into a neoshamanic vein of my own creation, based in part on the best of my experiences over time.

This book is one way in which I've tried to share some of these experiences with others. Animal totemism is often thought of as the domain of indigenous cultures, and these cultures do indeed have their own totemic systems. This book is geared more toward increasingly urban, technological, Western cultures that don't have inherent totemic systems anymore (beyond perhaps sports mascots and the like). It draws from a variety of wells of knowledge, from psychology to environmentalism to biology and more. And it reflects the individualistic background many spiritual seekers have been conditioned toward while also encouraging connection with community, particularly of a non-human sort.

Those who have read my previous books may notice some familiar elements here and there. While I have done my best to avoid recycling material (I believe every book needs to be its own entity), there are certain general concepts that need to be discussed here for context's purposes. I assure you this book is distinct from every other book I've written, and you haven't just laid hands on a rehash of older material. This book's goal is entirely different; I have continued to grow and change as a practitioner in the years since my previous publications, and have done my best to bring that through here. I do apologize if I seem a bit self-referential when I mention my other books as further reading, rather than unnecessarily repeating myself in this one.

I am always open for discussion about what I write. I appreciate constructive feedback, and I also spend entirely too much time on the Internet anyway. So feel free to email me or visit my website (addresses are in the About the Author section at the beginning of this book). I'm also available on Livejournal and Twitter as lupagreenwolf. I enjoy talking shop with people, so feel free to drop me a line!

—Lupa

Introduction

There is a misconception that "animal totemism" is universal, often based in some monolithic view of "Native American spirituality." It is more accurate to say that there are many totemisms, unique to each culture and region, and that there's no single right way to practice totemism. The various books already out there present their own unique approaches, from practices based in various cultures to more free-form systems authors have created from scratch.

New Paths to Animal Totems offers even more possibilities. I have taken the multiple threads I have woven together over the years to create my own way of relating to the totems, teasing them out into individual chapters. You may find that one approach rings more true to you than the rest, or you may end up creating your own unique blend from what's offered here.

One consideration that I would like you to keep in mind as you're reading and working through the material I offer is that this is a chance for you to practice totemism in a way that works best for you. Rather than trying to use the totemism of another culture and make it fit your own, I encourage you to work with totems in a way that helps you to become more fully yourself, no matter where you're coming from. This includes not only asking the totems for help with self-improvement, but also approaching them in a way that is most comfortable for you, respecting who you are and your life experiences. For example, if you're an urban dweller who has never had a chance to spend a night in the wilderness, you're not less able to work with totems than someone who's lived in the woods all their life. You can still have valid and rich relationships with the totems from where you're at.

To that end, everything in this book is designed to be used and adapted by people from many different walks of life. It is divided into three main sections. The first is an introduction to animal totemism; it includes information on what totems have meant to indigenous cultures around the world, as well how totemism has changed in recent years. I'll also discuss what animals can be totems, how many you can have, how to find them, and what to do once they've been found.

The second section is devoted to three different models (ways of understanding) animal totemism. The *Correspondences Model* uses directions, elements, and other patterns and correspondences to create a sort of totemic cosmology. This model creates a map to understand not just the totems associated with each direction, element, etc., but the qualities inherent to them. This is a good model if you tend to be a linear, left-brain thinker who likes a lot of organization and categorization, though it does leave plenty of room for creative personalization.

The *Bioregional Model* is an excellent choice for those wanting to have stronger relationships with the place where they live, and the beings with whom they share that place. Instead of totems from around the world like Cheetah or Panda Bear, the Bioregional Model draws the focus to a very small area, usually no more than a few hundred square miles at most. The totems of animals native to this area are given the most attention, and they are worked with not as disconnected spirits floating in a void someplace, but as members of a vibrant physical and spiritual ecosystem containing plants, waterways, land formations, and their own spirits and totems.

If the Bioregional Model is the most physically grounded, then the *Archetypal Model* is the most abstract. It plugs directly into the human psyche, both individually and by way of the collective unconscious, the part of our consciousness shared with other humans, inherited from our ancestors. In this model, totems represent different parts of human personality and experience, and can be worked with to better understand what it is to be human animals, as well as our relationships with other animals. This model may be very appealing if you value the saying "know thyself."

In addition to chapters outlining these three models, another gives some ideas on combining two or all three models. There's a lot of room for exploration and customization here. If you happen to really like elements of all three of the models, this chapter will help you find ways to put them together in a way that makes sense to you.

The final section of this book brings together a wealth of ideas for working with totems regardless of what model you use. Some of these can help you get to know a totem better; others let the totem help you with lessons you may need to learn, or by bringing about change in your life. The appendices include listings of animal-based nonprofit groups for those who wish to help the totems' physical counterparts, as well as a complete guided meditation that can be used for first meeting a totem and continuing communication over time.

These sections are meant to be read in order, as each section provides context for the next. As you read, take note of anything you may want to explore later. I also recommend reading the entire book before trying any exercises. This isn't because the exercises won't work if you try them beforehand; instead, reading the book as a complete work may give you a better idea of what I'm trying to show you overall. It may provide more of the purpose behind the exercises themselves, too.

If you get through the book and don't know what to do with what you've just read, that's okay. Think about which parts were really appealing and which you want to investigate. Look at the ones that might have been less clear and think of questions you may have about them.

One thing that may be helpful is to pick a model and try it on for size. You may know which one you'd like to start with, but if not, try choosing one at random. Feel free to do this with each of them in turn. There's no set time you need to spend with each, though I recommend at least a month of daily work given to each one, longer if you see fit.

I strongly recommend keeping a journal or other record of your impressions, questions, and experiences. I would especially like to draw your attention to any place where several questions are asked about the topic being discussed. These are woven in throughout the book to help inspire you to really dig into the concepts as well as to make better use of them. Look back through your notes and see what stood out to you the most—you may find more direction.

Finally, keep in mind that you don't need to have all the answers any time soon. I've talked to numerous people over the years who felt some frustration that they didn't really know what they believed and yearned for answers.

These answers are a form of valuable security, but the explorations you make in finding them can be just as incredible and are should not be missed. Start with what rings true to you, go from there, and modify your perspective as needed.

One

The Basics of Neopagan Totemism

"What are animal totems?"

This is a surprisingly loaded question without a single simple answer. Generally speaking, an animal totem is (usually) a nonphysical animal that offers its wisdom and guidance to human seekers. For example, a person whose totem is Honeybee may learn how to be more industrious or how to work together with other people for a common goal, while someone with Otter as a totem may learn to be more playful. Totems can also be associated with groups of people, such as families or tribes. Some animal-based surnames such as Wolf or Lamb may have their roots in old family totems or similar animal symbols. There are still cultures today that have family group totems, and the lore associated with these totems is passed from generation to generation.

Whether working with individuals or groups, totems help to bridge the increasing gap between humans and the rest of nature, reminding us that we are still a part of the natural cycles of this world. We are often so focused on members of our own species that we forget that our ancestors, as well as many indigenous people today, learn a lot from observing other animals, wild and domestic alike. Most of us are unable to spend a significant amount of time out in the woods or the desert, but totems remind us that no matter how deep into the city we go, we can still make the most of the lessons of our greater family of animals.

What is the basic nature of the totems themselves? What are they "made of"? Some will acknowledge great archetypal beings that embody all the qualities of a given animal—Bear as opposed to a bear spirit. Others see totems as individual animal spirits, and even give them (or ask for) particular names. And while many people see totems as spiritual beings that exist independently, others work with them as concepts within the psyche.

Who's correct? It's hard to say. Given that so much of spirituality is based on personal experience, absolute truth in these matters isn't something I suggest trying to pin down. However, let's look at a few contextual points, just to get an idea of where this all stems from in the first place.

In indigenous cultures, totems are traditionally collective, not individual. This means that rather than having your own totem, your entire family, clan, tribe, etc. would have one. In fact, totemism often started as a way to prevent people from marrying among their relatives; if a person had the same totem as you, you didn't get married. So in some cultures, the totem plays the role of embodied surname. This all weaves into the original meaning of the word *totem*, which derives from an Ojibwe root word concerning relationship with something or someone.[1]

In others, the relationship with one's totem is a lot more complex. There may be a series of extensive taboos surrounding certain behaviors involving the totem's physical counterparts—or not. A common example is a prohibition on eating the animal related to your totem, so if your totem is Whitetail Deer, you wouldn't eat deer meat. Taboos are not universal, of course; in some cultures eating your totem brings you closer to it, or the prohibition only covers certain parts of the animal.[2] Additionally, sometimes a totem would have a specific group within a culture that was dedicated to its honor and following; a good example of this is societies among the Oglala Lakota. The people

---

1. Claude Levi-Strauss, *Totemism* (Boston: Beacon Press, 1971).
2. Levi-Strauss, 1971; Nicholas J. Saunders, *Living Wisdom: Animal Spirits* (Boston: Little, Brown and Company, 1995).

in each society were expected to adhere to a set of standards of behavior and lifestyle associated with the animal totem of the society, and their function in the overarching community reflected that. The Wolf Society was one especially concerned with war and defense of the community, and the ideals that the members of that society followed trained them to be ready to fulfill that purpose.[3]

Totemism has historically been mostly associated with hunter-gatherer cultures, though it exists in a modified form in many agrarian cultures. In a hunter-gatherer context, the general relationship to animals and their totems has been one of cooperation and even worship, whereas in agrarian cultures the trend shifts more toward animals as either threats to crops, livestock to be used, or totems to be placated against the destruction of food sources.[4]

However, totemism has survived in other forms even as human societies have become more urbanized. It is uncertain whether European heraldry derived directly from earlier totemic beliefs, but the totemic elements of family and other group membership, as well as specific meanings associated with particular animals, may be found in heraldic symbolism.[5] Cultural rites such as the morris dances

---

3. Joseph Epes Brown, *Animals of the Soul: Sacred Animals of the Oglala Sioux* (Rockport, MA: Element Books, 1997).

4. Brian Morris, *The Power of Animals: An Ethnography* (Oxford: Berg, 1998).

5. Saunders, *Living Wisdom*.

of English tradition seem to have roots in older hunting rituals.[6] And modern sports teams and other groups use animals as group symbols, even if the meanings are relatively simple (i.e., "we're tough, bears are tough, so let's be the Bears!").

Which brings us to the conundrum of modern totemism: how do we take traditions that have largely been used in more rural, wild settings and make them relevant to twenty-first-century town and city living?

Introducing Neopagan Totemism

While there are plenty of indigenous cultures still alive and well, most of the people who tend to look for books on animal totemism are from postindustrial cultures that don't have an inherent totemic system, or have lost connection with ancestral totemic practices as a culture. We may refer to ourselves as Pagans, New Agers, earth religionists, witches, magicians, shamans, or any of a number of other terms. I have chosen the term "Neopagan totemism" to refer to modern, nonindigenous totemisms.

The term "Neopagan" is not meant to scare off anyone who may be of, say, a more Christian perspective. Rather, I'm using the term as it was imagined by its creator, the late Isaac Bonewits. He described a series of religious and

---

6. Evan John Jones and Chas Clifton, *Sacred Mask Sacred Dance* (St. Paul, MN: Llewellyn Publications, 1997).

spiritual movements stemming from the mid-twentieth century (and later) that were primarily designed to give new life to pre-Christian, often nature-based, religious practices and beliefs. These were categorized differently from older religions and spiritualities practiced by indigenous people, which Bonewits referred to as Paleopagan religions.[7] Since what I am presenting here is my own creation as a self-described white chick from the Midwest who has no indigenous connections beyond a few friendships, "Neopagan" applies to my system of totemism.

I would also consider Neopagan totemism to include totemic works by self-described Wiccans, witches, and Neopagans such as Ted Andrews and Yasmine Galenorn, and people more in the New Age crowd such as Jamie Sams and Dolfyn. There are also interpretations of various indigenous totemisms that deviate significantly enough from their roots to no longer be considered the original teachings, but are still effective, which could also be considered Neopagan. It's a broad umbrella of a term that for the purposes of this book should not be interpreted too strictly. Use it as shorthand, but if you prefer a different term, that's okay too.

One of my goals in creating this separate term is to demonstrate that there are plenty of differences between

---

7. Isaac Bonewits, "Defining Paganism: Paleo-, Meso-, and Neo-," 2007, accessed September 11, 2011 (http://www.Neopagan.net/PaganDefs.html).

what most of us who read and write books on animal totemism are doing, and what indigenous people have been doing for centuries (if not millennia). One of my greatest frustrations is that the actual traditions of indigenous cultures, particularly Native American cultures, have been buried under reams of paper about "Native American totemism" written not by tribe members, but by (usually white) non-Natives who take a smattering of traditions from a few cultures, toss in a whole lot of New Agery, and then call it genuinely Native.

Even presenting Native American practices as the main examples of indigenous totemisms still suggests that totemism is only found among those cultures. Describing totemism as "ancient knowledge" or "tribal practices" may lead the reader to believe that true totemic knowledge can only be gained from indigenous people, American or otherwise. This isn't to say that there isn't a wealth of knowledge and wisdom there; however, many people assume that nonindigenous cultures have nothing to contribute to totemism and nature spirituality in general. The concept of Neopagan totemism, therefore, was created in part to help break people out of the mindset that "totemism" = "Native American" or even "totemism" = "indigenous."

Some question using an Ojibwe-derived term to describe the practices of a wide variety of cultures, especially if the goal is to separate the automatic connection between totemism and Native Americans. *Totem* may have originated from the Ojibwe language, but just as *shaman* has long moved beyond its Siberian origins, so too has "totemism" come to apply to a variety of concepts in not only Ojibwe but other cultures as well. Thanks to Western anthropologists, it is the most familiar word used to describe the various sorts of animal and other natural beings that people around the world have worked with, and so it is often simpler to just use the term as shorthand rather than describing each individual culture's system in its own words. This in no way should be seen as a suggestion to see all of these unique and varied systems as one monolithic entity but rather in the same way that the terms "religion" or "spirituality" describe many diverse systems of belief.

There is also some debate over traditional versus non-traditional methods of learning and practicing totemism. Some people feel that it's best to work within an established set of traditions that have been developed over time, with others to teach and support you. There are indigenous communities that have opened up a portion of their cultural and spiritual practices, to include totemism, to others.

However, many people have found success in creating their own relationships with the totems, without the structure of an existing tradition. Plenty of us have been self-taught, and have worked from our own cultural perspectives no matter what they may be. We've learned from books, websites, or sheer trial and error, and our efforts have worked for us.

Really, what it comes down to is what works best for you. If you read through this and perhaps other books as well and find that you still yearn for more traditional guidance, then keep aiming your explorations in that direction. If you find some value in what you read here and elsewhere, make the most of it for your own practice.

With that set of definitions and concepts out of the way, let's get to more of the nuts and bolts of Neopagan totemism.

What Animals Can Be Totems?

If you look at most books on totemism, they tend heavily toward what I call the BINABM—Big, Impressive North American Birds and Mammals. Some of this has to do with the aforementioned tendency to equate totemism with native North American cultures and therefore North American animals. And because we tend to be anthropocentric, we favor animals more like us, which makes mammals the most popular, followed by birds, then other vertebrates, and finally the often-ignored invertebrate kingdom. Finally, we like what are known as charismatic megafauna—basically, big animals that we think are really, really cool.

You're going to see a lot about Wolf, Deer, Bear, Eagle, Hawk, maybe Snake, and Turtle, and perhaps even

Butterfly and Bee. However, unless you get a totem animal dictionary written by someone trying to include more animals than anyone else, you're not likely to run across entries for Platypus, Sea Slug, or Rotifer. Oddly enough, very few people work with primate totems of any sort. This may be because they resemble us so closely that we may feel we don't have a lot to learn from them, instead wanting to connect with a more exotic "other" being. This is a shame, as we can learn a great deal about ourselves from our cousins on the great Tree of Life, as well as the less common animals, and even the ones we can't easily see with the naked eye.

Indeed, all animals have totems. In my experience, at least, a totem is the intermediary between a given species and the rest of the world. This is especially important for us as humans, as we have quite often been taught that we are separate from the rest of the world and are "unnatural." Working with totems is a great way to remind us that we are still animals and are still of nature, even if we don't perceive ourselves as such. One of the earliest lessons Gray Wolf taught me was the joys and benefits of getting outdoors more and "taking my inner wolf for a run," as it were. Those early experiences in my backyard, open lots, and little patches of scrub forest were integral to my later connections to the land, as well as environmental efforts. Gray Wolf showed me from a young age that I was an integral part of my environment, and that I had an effect on and was affected by it.

Note, too, that I mention Gray Wolf and not just Wolf; in my experience, each species has a totem. I have found that Gray Wolf and Red Wolf are two different beings, and the same with Black Bear, Brown Bear, and Polar Bear. Since a totem is "made of" the behavior, physical characteristics, and observations of the physical animals, different totems will reflect what is unique about their species, as well as what they have in common with similar animals. Some people still prefer to work with a more generic Bear or Wolf; this is personal preference. From here on out, I will primarily be referring to totems as species-specific.

Some totems are more likely to work with us than others. Gray Wolf is very popular. Some would say it's because wolves are considered "cool" these days. However, I and others feel it's also that Gray Wolf tries to reach out to a number of people and is more willing than just about any other totem to interact with humans.[8] After all, part of that intermediary work doesn't just involve humans telling the totems what they need, but the totems also telling humans what the animals need! (Again, this will be expanded upon later.)

---

8. Ravenari, "Wolf Teacher Give-Away," n.d., accessed September 11, 2011 (http://www.wildspeak.com/totems/wolf.html).

The other factor is you. Just because you find a particular totem appealing doesn't mean the feeling is mutual. Totems have personalities, though because of the nature of their being—which is rather broad, expansive, and informed by a variety of information and experiences—their notion of "personality" is a bit different from our own. This is why some people feel more comfortable working with an individual animal spirit as opposed to totems, which experience the lives, deaths, and afterlives of countless animal spirits. Beyond that, a totem may feel that you are not ready to work with it, or even that it has nothing for you to work with.

———

A totem's readiness (or not) to work with you leads me to a common trend: many people will choose, whether consciously or not, one of the BINABM as their totem. If a totem that wants to work with someone is less conspicuous, the person may go a long time without realizing that the reason he or she isn't getting results is because he or she is talking to the wrong critter! Some people feel ashamed of the idea of having Cottontail Rabbit or Banana Slug as a totem, and so try their very hardest to get Bald Eagle or American Elk to like them. Fortunately, a good number of these people come around and eventually accept that while they may not have the most impressive totems, they've found ones that help them the most.

Naturally, it follows to question whether one can choose a totem or whether the totem must always choose you. Most people will say the latter; a lot of this is because they're trying to discourage the aforementioned practice of overlooking less impressive totems and choosing BINABM instead. It is possible to initiate contact with a totem, though, and develop the relationship over time. It requires you to be very honest with yourself about your reasons for connecting with that particular animal, and the totem may decide that your reasons aren't quite on target. However, it isn't unheard of for someone to choose a totem without it becoming a matter of "flavor of the week."

Charity has always loved seagulls, even if other people think they're irritating pests. She likes the way they fly and their "singing" cries. After learning about totemism, she decides that she wants to work with Ring-Billed Gull because she admires these birds so much. In meditation, she approaches Ring-Billed Gull and asks him to consider being her totem. She tells him how she appreciates the resourcefulness of gulls and their ability to move on land, water, and air currents. Since Charity feels she is a pretty resourceful person herself, she feels kinship with the gulls. Ring-Billed Gull agrees, but only if she commits to working with him for at least a year, and part of her work includes educating people about the ecological niche that gulls fill and why they aren't just pests. Charity indeed keeps up her end of the bargain, and the lessons she has learned from Ring-Necked Gull have only strengthened their bond. She looks forward to another year of working with Gull energy!

There is also some question as to whether or not extinct or mythological animals can be totems. In my experience, this is primarily an issue of semantics and perspective. I have worked with beings that are totemic in nature that are mythological/fantastic (think Unicorn or Basilisk), and I have also done a good deal of work with extinct totems, from various dinosaurs to Dodo Bird. Because these totems don't have children on the physical plane any more (or at all), their perspective on what's going on here is a bit different, especially if the animals have been extinct for a good long while. However, they can still work with us in the same way as those that most people would think of as totems. Whether you choose to use the word *totem* to describe all of these, or only those totems who have children alive and well on this plane today, is up to you.

A final note: you may notice I use a variety of pronouns when speaking of individual totems. In my experience, animal totems are neither wholly male nor wholly female. In species of animal that are sexually dimorphic— that is, the physical animals are generally either male or female—the totem of that species may show up as either female or male, or may carry the energy of both. I have had Whitetail Deer show up as a buck, a doe, an antlered doe, and a hermaphroditic deer expressing both male and female traits and physiology. There are many species, especially (though not exclusively) invertebrates that are also hermaphroditic, asexual, or can even change sex at some point in their lives.

So to an extent, my use of female or male pronouns when referring to a specific totem (such as Blue Whale or Cleaner Wrasse) is somewhat arbitrary, based mainly on how each totem has most commonly presented itself to me. If I am speaking of a generic singular totem, I'll often use the term "it," not to objectify the totem, but as a simple gender-neutral word.

Are Totems Dangerous?

This may seem like a silly question to ask, given how many books there are out there extolling the virtues of animal totems and their ability to help us. However, totems are strongly influenced by the type of animal they are, and not every animal is safe to be around! Coyote, for example, is infamous for being a trickster, and the tricks aren't always in our favor, nor are they always benign. Some totems can be outright hostile; when I tried visiting Dodo in a journey, I ended up being chased away by a very angry avian totem! As with approaching any spiritual being, be respectful to the point of caution (especially the first time) and don't assume that the totem has anything to teach you or even wants to acknowledge you.

We tend to focus a lot on what totems can do for us, but it's also valuable to consider what we can do for them in return. In addition to humans, totems also interact with other species and, most importantly, their own physical counterparts. I have found that their first priority tends to be their children here on Earth, and more than one totem has come to me for help protecting those animals through donations, volunteering, or political action and awareness-raising.

Additionally, spiritual work in general can stress your psyche, especially if you're not used to sometimes-intense altered states of consciousness. Any ritual that works will shift your consciousness in some manner, sometimes temporarily, but sometimes leaving a small but significant permanent change in your worldview (which is often one intended purpose, especially with things like rites of passage). This change can have healing effects for psychic and energetic ailments, as well as strengthening one's mental and emotional reserves. It should not, however, be seen as a replacement for any sort of psychological or other medical treatment, simply a complement.

How Many Do I Get?

How many totems a person has depends on whom you ask. Here are just a few of the responses I've heard people try to give as an across-the-board answer for everyone:

- One totem per person

- Two totems, one each for left/right, male/female, dark/light, etc.

- Four totems, one for each of the cardinal directions

- Five totems, for the cardinal directions plus center

- Six totems, for the cardinal directions plus up and down

- Seven totems, for the cardinal directions, up, down and center

- Nine totems, including the cardinal directions, plus up, down, left, right, and within

While each of these is a valid system, each person's experience is different, and what I have seen most commonly with people, particularly those who have been working with totems for a decent amount of time, is that the number each person has at any time is organic. Some totems stick around for life; others may come and go. Some people are able to create relationships of varying intensities with many different totems; others only work with a very small number, often very closely.

If you're at all familiar with my other writings on totemism, you may see references to primary, secondary, and tertiary totems. The following is a system I came up with for my own convenience. It's a way to categorize the totems in my life by their general roles:

- Primary totems are what most people think of as totems. They're your life totems, the ones who are around for most, if not all, of your life.

  Richard has long been referred to as "Bear" by his friends. It fits, too, given that he's a big, burly guy with a full, brown beard. Though powerful and not someone you want to pick on, he's also a good person to have around in the woods since he knows his way around pretty well, and has a lot of wilderness skills. It came as no surprise when a few years ago Brown Bear showed up during a totemic meditation; Richard could tell where Brown Bear's influence had been earlier in his life, and since then he's learned even more about himself and his totem.

- Secondary totems come into your life of their own volition, either to teach you a particular lesson, ask for your help with something pretty involved, or simply to be with you during a particular stage of your life.

Wendy is having a tough time dealing with her divorce. It has been an ugly situation, and now she just wants to move through it. While she's known her primary totem has been Red Fox for many years, she is a bit surprised when Fox steps back and allows Leopard to take his place. Over the course of the next year, Leopard teaches Wendy more about herself and her own strengths, as well as how to find solace in solitude. Like a leopard relaxing in a tree, she finds more ways to take a break from her situation and have some time to deal with things, while also staying alert to what's going on around her. A year later, she is a stronger, happier person and has successfully put the past behind her. Leopard bids her a fond farewell, and Red Fox resumes his usual place in her life.

· Tertiary totems are ones you go to for help with specific situations, such as help with a spell or ritual, and the relationship rarely goes beyond that.

Eliza is looking for a job; unfortunately, it's been a few months and there have been few nibbles. She decides to add a little extra "oomph" to her efforts with a ritual to send out her intent into the world. She would like some help getting that energy where it needs to be, and so she contacts Pigeon. She thinks that Pigeon can help, being an urban totem close to many of the places she would like to work, and also for the bird's heritage as a carrier of messages. Pigeon agrees to help, and together they perform a ritual to raise energy meant to bring work to Eliza, with Pigeon carrying the energy to where it needs to be. Eliza continues her job-hunting efforts and soon has a number of interviews, one of which results in her getting a great job. Eliza thanks Pigeon for the help, and keeps a small pigeon feather on her desk to remind her of that aid.

Note that I did not say that you have to have a specific number of any of these types of totem. Not everyone will have totems of all sorts. Some people do, for example, lack primary totems. There is absolutely nothing wrong with you if this is the case; it just may be that you're going to have totems who are more temporary throughout your life. And others only ever work with their primary, deepening that connection over time.

I have had numerous secondary and tertiary totems, though Gray Wolf seems to have been my only *lifelong* primary. I (and others) have also had the nature of a totemic relationship change over time, such as a tertiary totem deciding to stick around longer and become more of a secondary or even primary. Red Fox, for example, initially showed up in my life in 2004 to help balance out some of Gray Wolf's more aggressive traits. After she did her intended work with me during that year, she decided to stick around, and came to represent the direction of south and change in my life. She started out as a secondary totem, meaning only to help me through a year of change, and instead took on a more permanent role.

Your mileage may vary, and don't take my or anyone else's experience as something for you to measure up to. *Any organizational system, no matter whose, shouldn't be seen as the ultimate authority on how many totems you should or shouldn't have.*

How Do I Find My Totem?

This is probably the most common question people ask when they first find out about animal totems. I chose to explain in detail what totems were first, so that you had some idea of what you were actually looking for.

There are people, and I include myself in this group, who simply know from an early age who their totems are. When I was a very young child, I looked out our back patio one day. Gray Wolf chose that moment to make himself known to me through the German shepherd dog we had at the time, who was looking uncharacteristically feral in that moment. It may have been only childish imagination, but it served as an introduction, and the relationship has been strong ever since.

If you are not one of these people, it's okay. It doesn't mean you're less spiritually attuned. It just means that you may need a little more structure in your search to find your totem. Give yourself some time to familiarize yourself with totemism through this book as well as any other resources you see fit, and see if you gravitate toward any particular model. In this process you may find that a totem makes itself known to you. Alternatively, once you're more grounded in the theoretical knowledge, you may find that one of the following methods helps you to make that first contact.

Guided Meditation: This is my personal favorite. Guided meditation is essentially visualizing with an intent and often a bare-bones script of where you're going to go in the meditation. The one provided in Appendix A will help you get to a place where you can meet a totem. It allows you the freedom to interact with that totem as long as you both want, without a particular time allotted or agenda given. Guided meditation is one of the most free-form methods because you can meet any totem in meditation, and you can also have control over your choices and what you say to the totem. You can use it to meet a totem for the first time, and you can also use it for continued communication and work.

Some books on totemism talk about journeying to find your totem(s). I differentiate between guided meditation and a proper shamanic journey. In the former, you are using a script; generally, a guided meditation takes you to a neutral place where you can meet with spiritual beings, and the entire experience is relatively safe. A journey, on the other hand, is not at all scripted;

it takes you into the spirits' own territory (often deep inside), and it can be very spiritually and psychically dangerous. Injuries and illnesses sustained in journeying may even manifest psychosomatically as mental or physical health problems back in the waking world.

Sandy sits in a quiet field on a sunny morning, facing east. She relaxes and closes her eyes, and then imagines that she is flying farther into the east. As she does, the scenery begins to change, becoming colored with a golden light, and soft breezes carry her ever farther. Before her she can see an animal, and as she approaches she sees it is a white stag with gold horns. Stag stands before her, greets her with a bow of his antlered head, and says, "What would you know?" She speaks with him a while, and then speaks her promise to greet him any time she greets the east, and to visit him often in this place to learn more of what he has to teach her. Then she returns to her home and begins to draw a picture of this totem to place on the east side of her altar.

Dreams: Contrary to popular belief, not every animal sighting in a dream is significant. Most dreams are simply the brain's way of organizing the events of the day, and because this has more to do with your unconscious mind, there's a lot of speaking in symbols. Generally speaking, an animal in a dream is most likely just a symbol the brain is coming up with to represent something entirely different. However, on occasion you may have a Big Dream, one that you know is different without a doubt. In that case, I generally suggest using guided meditation to go talk to the relevant totem to find out whether or not there was indeed any message there.

Some people will deliberately seek a totem through dreams, sometimes doing a prayer or small ritual before sleeping to try to invite Big Dreams. This can be as simple as an affirmation like "I will open my dreams to my totem tonight," or as elaborate as a multilayered ritual done periodically to keep the welcoming energy going.

Brian normally has fairly quiet dreams. But tonight, his dreams are restless and energetic; in them he is searching—but for what? He finds himself on the jogging path he runs down several times a week, only this time it is the middle of the night instead of his customary afternoon. He continues down the well-worn trail, and as he turns a corner, he finds himself surrounded by fireflies—millions of them lighting up the night like golden stars! He is so fascinated that he stops in his tracks, and he feels as though the blinking, shining lights are almost creating a pattern. But what does it mean? He awakens, and resolves to find out more about these little glowing insects that fill his yard every summer, and why they suddenly seem so important.

Animal Sightings: As with dreams, most of the time when you see an animal, there's no real significance to it other than getting to see another living being in its element. People often forget that animals don't exist for our pleasure and interpretation; they simply *are*. So, for example, if you keep seeing hawks in your yard, even if you hadn't seen them before, chances are a breeding pair has taken up residence nearby, and the only significance is that your yard happens to be in *their* territory. Also, as with dreams, if it feels really significant, you may do well to go talk to the totem in question and see if there's anything going on other than having a nonhuman neighbor.

Up until a few weeks ago, Devon had never seen an armadillo in real life. But lately they've been showing up all over the place! Armadillos expanding their range north had begun to make occasional appearances on the outskirts of her town (and, sadly, as roadkill that she had seen a couple of times on her drive to work). A local barbecue restaurant had opened up a couple of months ago, and had an armadillo as a mascot. And just today, she went to her favorite antique shop and saw an old basket made of an armadillo's shell. Devon feels that all these armadillos aren't a coincidence and so she decides to research them more, and maybe even see if the totem Armadillo might be interested in talking to her about it all.

Totem Cards: To me, this is the most limiting method of finding a totem. I only do readings for suggesting tertiary totems to querents, and even then it's with the knowledge that the deck I use only has so many animals. Every deck that has specific animals is necessarily limited, and if your totem happens not to be an animal in that deck, you may end up with misidentification. Still, if you're just looking for a likely candidate to help you with a specific problem, this may be a good, quick solution.

If you do want to use cards with more versatility, I attempted to address the problem of "too many animals, not enough cards to go around" with a deck of my own design. It uses a combination of guided meditation and cards that signify things like habitats, animal taxonomy, and other traits rather than specific species of animal. It's designed to help you get into contact with any animal totem at all, from Amoeba to Blue Whale, and I describe in detail how to make and use the deck yourself in my book *DIY Totemism: Your Personal Guide to Animal Totems*.

When Elliot brought home the deck of animal cards from the local metaphysical shop, he figured he'd get some mighty, powerful animal like Wolf or Elk. So when he drew the card for Snail, he felt a bit disappointed. However, the author had written about how all animal totems have their own strengths, not just the obviously big and strong ones. Then Elliot remembered that his boss had suggested he take some of his unused vacation time, as she was concerned that he had been pushing himself too hard at work. Maybe slowing down and being more Snail-like wasn't such a bad idea after all.

A Quick Note on Totem Communication

All of these are ways to introduce you to the totem. But what if you've never communicated with a totem or other spirit before? How do you know that you've actually made contact? How do you know that you aren't just talking to yourself?

Let's say that you're doing one of the rituals that I describe in this book to help you talk to a totem. You've called to the totem, and now you're waiting to see if it responds.

Sometimes the result is something fairly obvious. You may notice a change in the temperature of the room, or a breeze that seems to come out of nowhere. Quite often, you may not observe anything physically, but you may feel, hear, and see things with your mind's eye and other nonphysical senses, like getting the feeling that you're no longer alone.

You may even find that the totem or other spirit decides to strike up a conversation right then and there. I often "hear" the totems "inside" of me; it's not so much actual words as it is feelings and impressions that translate themselves into words, if that makes sense. And it is quite easily discernible from the voices of physical people around me.

Give yourself time to observe what happens inside and around you once you've invited the totems in. Don't make any judgments; simply write things down as they happen or as soon as you're done with the entire ritual. Even if you don't seem to have any totems show up or even notice anything out of the ordinary, write down how you feel in that moment. Those feelings may end up being the signs you use to tell when a totem has arrived.

Getting to Know You

Usually when people find their totems (in Neopagan totemism, anyway), the first thing they do is get a totem dictionary or three and look up what the totem supposedly "means." The thing to keep in mind is that every dictionary is based primarily on the interpretations of the totem that the author thinks are important, whether based in history or in his or her own experiences with the totem. When you buy a totem animal dictionary, you're basically buying someone else's thoughts on a totem. This is not necessarily a bad thing; a dictionary can be a way to at least get an idea of what a relationship with a totem can look like. However, I tend to discourage people from assuming that what a totem told such-and-such author is automatically going to be what the totem tells them.

Even keywords like "teacher" for Gray Wolf or "healer" for Brown Bear can be interpreted in very different ways depending on the person and circumstance.

Therefore, I propose a few alternatives to going out and buying every totem dictionary you can find to try and amass the greatest amount of someone else's thoughts:

Natural History: Totemic lore is very often based on human observations of animal behavior. For example, the pack cooperation of gray wolves in the hunt led to Gray Wolf being associated with, among other things, hunting parties in many indigenous North American cultures. And Brown Bear most likely got a reputation as a healer because brown bears are omnivorous and spend a great deal of time eating roots, berries, and other plant material, much of which is medicinal. Since the bears know where to find these things, Brown Bear became associated with the knowledge of these plants all around.

You can in a way "reverse engineer" totemic lore by going back to animal behavior, physiology, and how the animal interacts with the environment. Keep in mind that this all hinges on your interpretation of what you observe. Whether you are watching the animals in person, on YouTube videos, or reading books and articles, you're going to be filtering the information through your perceptions and thought patterns, and this subjectivity is going to have a lot to do with what information and traits stand out to you the most.

Mythology and Folklore: This tends to be a more collective gnosis than a single author's book, built up over time and generations. It's still someone else's interpretation on a cultural level, but it's worth taking a look at. Keep in mind, too, that mythology doesn't have to be old. People are creating mythology every day; we simply call it "fiction." Granted, some people consider fiction created in a trance state to be more "genuine" than the rest, but all mythology got its start in more or less the same way, through storytelling traditions.[9]

Guided Meditation: Again, this is a favored technique of mine. Communicating directly with the totem is the most effective way to get personal information on what the totem has to say to you. If all you do is hear about a totem, read its entry in a dictionary, and then assume that's your totem, it's like seeing an attractive person, asking an acquaintance for their impression of them, and then declaring that person your new

---

9. For more information on pop culture as modern mythology, the works of Taylor Ellwood are a good start, particularly *Pop Culture Magick* and *Multi-media Magic* (Megalithica Books, 2004 and 2008, respectively). Also, some fiction authors are especially notable for the mythological structure and quality of their works; Neil Gaiman, Octavia Butler, Jane Yolen, and Charles de Lint are just a few better-known examples.

significant other, all without ever consulting them. Sounds silly, but it happens all the time! My advice every time someone asks, "Is this animal my totem?" is "Go to the totem, not me, and ask for yourself."

Other People: Not that talking to other people has no value, of course. While technically reading a book on totems is consulting that author for his or her opinion in a static, page-limited format, there are numerous other ways to talk shop with fellow totem fans. You can go to workshops held locally, at Pagan or New Age shops and other events, ones aimed at informing people more about totems. And as long as you have an Internet connection, there are plenty of forums that either have a subforum for discussing totemism and related topics, or are entirely dedicated to that material. Just be aware that people can say anything they like, and it's helpful to have that proverbial grain of salt handy to gauge how much to believe something someone says. As with books, there are plenty of people pretending to have authority in certain cultures they don't actually have. Be wary whenever someone is talking about, for example, "Native American spirituality" without making references to specific tribes. (A great resource for finding out more about legitimate and fraudulent people posing as Native American elders and related folk is New Age Frauds and Plastic Shamans, located at http://www .newagefraud.org).

Initial Work with Totems

This chapter is intended to lay a lot of groundwork for totemic work. It includes basic information such as what totems are, how you can interact with them, and so on. Don't just take my word for it, though. It's good to take time to digest what you've read and figure out what you think and feel about it. To that end, I've included a few exercises to help you process this chapter and gather more information about totemism.

You may complete the first three exercises now, before you continue in the book, or you can save them for later. They're good for brainstorming ideas and collecting information so you can identify what you already know, as well as questions you may have. I would recommend saving the fourth one, which involves actually trying to find totems, for when you have read through the rest of this book. Later chapters include more information that may be very helpful for actually practicing totemism rather than simply thinking about it.

- Write an essay or journal entry about what you currently know about totems, what you think they are, and how they may interact with human beings, other animals, the environment, etc. Do you agree with everything you've read or heard about them? What do you feel may be the most important ways for you, personally, to get totemic information?

Write about what stands out, but perhaps also make note of things that don't seem important right now; they may end up being relevant later.

- If you do know at least one totem, write down everything you know about it, what it has told you, what lore surrounds it, etc. You can also write down things you might ask it next time you meet, as well as any requests it may have had of you, and whether or not you've been able to fulfill those yet.

- Pick a few books or other resources from the bibliography and read them. Try to vary their subject material; rather than picking all books on Neopagan totemism or historical perspectives, maybe get one of each and then one or two other resources not related to totemism alone.

- If you don't know any of your totems, or want to meet new ones, try at least one of the methods mentioned above. If you don't get results right away, give it some time; the totem may not feel ready, or may not feel you are yet prepared.

Two

Before We Move On ...

The next few chapters describe different models of understanding and working with animal totems. There are two primary reasons I'm introducing readers to alternate models of totemism: breaking the cultural mold, and the importance of structure.

It may feel as though you've stepped into a completely different book in this short chapter; there's very little on animal totems and a whole lot more about the people who work with them. But this will be importantwhen you get into the rest of the text. The previous chapter was an introduction to what totems may bring into your life. This one is more about what you bring to the table yourself. Who you are as a person may affect your work with the totems. It is a more abstract, cerebral set of things to consider, but they will matter once we get into the practical stuff beginning in the next chapter.

Breaking the Cultural Mold

The most common model of Neopagan totemism is a pseudoindigenous (often pseudo–Native American) format that tosses around words like "medicine" and "power" and "shamanic." Often a selection of customs and beliefs from various Native American cultures are invoked as examples; alternately, if the totemic system being described is more culturally specific, such as Celtic cultures, then lore and practices from those cultures will be examined in detail.

I want to break out of the trend of being so fixated on doing things like people of another culture, instead offering more open-source ideas that are consciously informed by my own experiences as a middle-class white chick from the midwestern United States. That said, these ideas are open to anyone who wants to make use of them. There's a misconception a lot of Americans have that "American culture" is largely shopping malls, fast food, and "reality" television.[10] While these are certainly very common ele-

---

10. Disclaimer: Never having been a part of any other culture, I can only really speak to my experiences and observations of over thirty years living in the United States. I have readers around the world, though, who have connected with my works, and so it's my hope that this book, too, will find similar international acceptance. However, please be aware that some of my writing and examples may be very America-centric.

ments of American popular culture, they are hardly the only elements of nonindigenous American experience.[11]

For one thing, there are a lot of people who can be considered "American"; we are less a melting pot where everything loses its unique flavor and more a salad with distinct components in close quarters. Unfortunately, the media (and not just news) largely portrays white, English-speaking Americans as the dominant culture in the United States, forgetting that the values and core cultural identity of many Americans, whether white or people of color, may vary drastically from that corporate-heavy image. Therefore, many people—Americans and otherwise—assume assume malls and reality TV are the only elements of American culture available to them.

Additionally, a commonly cited reason many white Americans in particular try to seek out Native American, Celtic, and other cultures' spiritual practices is because they feel that since they've rejected the malls and

---

11. Please note the use of "nonindigenous American." Indigenous American tribes are a whole other constellation of cultures that have much deeper roots in the land here than immigrant cultures from the past few hundred years, and so when I am discussing American culture here I am primarily referring to the layer of American culture predominantly—though certainly not exclusively—shaped by hundreds of years of Western European immigration. Admittedly, this sidesteps the very involved and politically charged debate of what it means to be an "American," which is a discussion for another book. My speaking of this particular culture should not in any way be taken as stating it is the only relevant culture in this country.

fast food and such, they are "without culture." This is impossible; we can never be completely culturally neutral, and in fact the *idea* of being "culturally neutral" is in itself a cultural artifact. Our cultural background is ingrained into us from a very young age and shapes the very context in which we understand the world. The way we speak, the patterns of our thoughts, the motivations and impulses that lead us to explore new paths—all these are remnants of the cultures we were raised in, whether we want to admit it or not. Shopping malls and fast food are just symptoms of the culture that created them; they are not the culture itself.

I want to encourage people to break out of the pseudo-indigenous trend in totemism, and instead explore what they themselves bring as individuals. There's a concept known as one's *social location:* this describes your place in society, not just your geographic location. It's a way of understanding your identity and including where you could know yourself more thoroughly. Since you influence your spirituality simply by being a participant, knowing your social location can help you understand where your own social and cultural background affects your path. Here are a few elements of personal identity that can make up your social location:

- Race/ethnicity (can include important semantic discussions such as identifying as "black" instead of "African-American")

- Physical sex (male, female, intersex, etc.)

- Gender identity (cisgender—identifying with the physical sex you were born as; transgender—identifying with a physical sex other than what you were born as; genderqueer or genderfluid—not necessarily adhering to any single gender identity)

- Sexual orientation (heterosexual, homosexual, bisexual, pansexual, asexual, etc.)

- Physical health and ability/challenges (including living with chronic illnesses and disabilities, both visible and invisible)

- Culture(s), location, and spirituality(s) of origin (and whether you still identify with these)

- Current culture(s) and location, and spirituality if you have it (and how these may differ from earlier ones in your life)

- Socioeconomic status and level of income (also can include social attitudes toward your profession)

- Educational background (level of education, quality of education, consistent access to education, literacy)

- Family structure (nuclear, extended, nontraditional, with or without children, biological/married into/adopted/chosen)

- Political identity, not just limited to formal political parties

· Immigration/native status (what generation immigrant, native background, immigrant ancestral relationship to native populations and to the land itself, reasons for immigration)

My Social Location

Take some time to think about your social location using the categories above. How do you feel you identify in each of these cases? How much have you thought about these parts of your identity? How important are they, or are there any that don't really matter to you? Do you feel there are any other parts of your identity not listed here that may be important to you? Do you feel these may affect your work with animal totems at all, or your approach to spirituality in general?

───────

You don't have to have all the answers to do the work in this book; they only serve as food for thought that may help you get a better understanding of yourself and your relationship to the world—a big part of spirituality in general. Your answers can help you understand why you believe what you believe, or even figure out beliefs if you're feeling like a spiritual wanderer. And, with regards to totemism, knowing your social location can help you develop your personal model of totemism, whether it's one described in this book, or one of your own unique creation. Instead of trying to be like someone from another culture, you can be who you are more fully and consciously.

The Importance of Structure

Another question may be: why introduce the models here, just when I've finished describing how to meet and bond with your totem before getting into the real meat of ritual practices? Doesn't it make more sense to go directly from "Here's what a totem is" to "Whee! It's time to start working with totems!"? The simple answer is structure. While I am a huge fan of off-the-cuff, unstructured spiritual and magical practice, I also value structure as a tool for exploration and understanding.

Everyone has their own preference for structure or the lack thereof. Those who are new to this whole totemism thing may find it helpful to have a sort of scaffolding on which to build their conception of what totemism is. More experienced people may appreciate having alternative viewpoints to explore and compare to their existing knowledge. Some people may appreciate having these frameworks to hang onto—and modify—as we get into the practical work with totems later in this book.

Each of these models has been extrapolated from my years of experience working with totems. They're all based on the same essential material, but each one approaches totemism from a different angle, highlighting some elements of my practice while downplaying others. As one example, both the Bioregional Model, which is very external, and the Archetypal Model, which is more internal, are integral parts of my overall practice; I have simply drawn them out individually for more careful study and exploration.

My own personal blend of these models is just one way to use the material I'm providing. You may find that one of the models here really speaks to you and adopt it as your personal way of relating to totems. Or you may be inspired to create by what I offer here, and take what's useful from one or more models to build your own pathway. Either way, please think of these models not as strict dogma, but as suggested material to be used as you see fit. The next three chapters are full of tools you can use as you're forming your own relationships with the animal totems you work with.

What's Next?

Each of the next three chapters will outline one of these models of totemism—the Correspondences Model, the Bioregional Model, and the Archetypal Model. I've provided enough theoretical material to give a decent amount of background on the origins and reasons behind each model, along with plenty of practical exercises and rituals so you can try the models out for yourself. In addition, there's a fourth chapter all about ways to combine these models if you so choose.

As I mentioned previously, my recommendation is that you read through the remainder of the book before trying anything out. This way, you'll have a more complete view of everything you can choose. I'd also recommend experimenting with one single model at a time before trying to combine them. This way you have more of an idea of what each model has to offer on its own, and you have a more thorough understanding of how it functions as a stand-alone practice. It's like learning to use acrylic paints, woodworking, and polymer clay as individual artistic media before combining them into a more complex mixed-media piece. You may find that you like a particular model well enough as it is, but if you do decide to combine elements of more than one model, you'll have a better understanding of the strengths and limitations of each.

Three

The Correspondences Model of Totemism

The title of this chapter is a bit misleading. Rather than presenting just one overarching model, as in the next two chapters, this one is going to present several different systems, each using a different set of correspondences for its basic structure. Correspondences are sets of qualities that are often related to each other; this chapter will focus primarily on spiritual and magical correspondences.

Astrology is a well-known example of a set of correspondences. Looking at the popular Western zodiac, each astrological sign is associated with a particular constellation of stars and a period of time in the year lasting about a month. There are also certain personality traits said to be found in people who were born when the sun, moon, or various planets were in a particular sign. For example, if the sun was in Scorpio when you were born, you may be a very passionate yet secretive person with a strong interest in hidden spiritual matters. So the constellation, the time period between October 23 and November 22, qualities like secrecy and passion—and, of course, the scorpion—are just some of the correspondences associated with Scorpio.

Within the Correspondences Model of totemism, you are finding totems that match a particular set of qualities that often go together. You might work with a different totem for each month of the year, or each of the cardinal directions. There are divination decks, such as the Ted Andrews *Animal-Wise* deck, that combine the traditional seventy-eight cards of the tarot with animal totems. Totem animal dictionarie—such as books written by authors like Andrews, Steven Farmer, and Susie Green, and websites such as Wildspeak.com—often pass along common qualities of totems that many people have observed, such as Gray Wolf being a totem of teaching, or Wolverine being associated with ferocity and gluttony.

Your work with the totems doesn't have to be strictly limited by the constraints of a given correspondence system; you can think of it as a starting point. Knowing, for example, that Gray Wolf is often associated with teaching doesn't tell you what Wolf will teach you, or even if that's how he wants to work with you. He may be more of a protector in your life, or a facilitator of social experiences.

What's important about whatever set of correspondences you work with is that it does provide you with a beginning. Especially when they're new to totemism, many people like having some ideas to get them started to learn the basics and then explore from there. That's the beauty of correspondences—you can work with what others have already built up over the years, and add your own embellishments as you see fit.

You can even put together your own set of personal correspondences, though that's a more advanced practice than using a preexisting system. For now, I'll discuss some sets of correspondences that are well-established. This is for much the same reason I suggested reading this book all the way through before trying the practices—context. If you can see the methods and mechanics of how totems can be combined with existing systems of correspondence, you have a more thorough set of tools for creating your own unique structure.

Personally, I like starting with preexisting sets of correspondences and then adding my own meaning. One structure I really like is the four cardinal directions—north, east, south, and west. I like the fairly common correspondences associated with them in general Neopaganism, such as elements (earth, air, fire, water) and seasons (winter, spring, summer, fall). But these have personal meaning as well; for example, Gray Wolf is my totem of the north, and helps to ground me (earth). Winter is not my favorite season because it's cold, but the quiet time as plants and animals rest gives me much-needed space to meditate on silence and rest, something that helps with that grounding process.

Correspondences are not always static, unchanging things. You may find that regardless of what system you use, some of the totems may change over time, and it's important to pay attention when this happens. For example, if you're working within the directional system, you may start out with Golden Eagle as your totem of the east, but at some point later, Eagle steps aside and House Sparrow takes her place.

If this occurs, it may be a sign that things are shifting in your life. If you associate east with air and intellectual pursuits, it may be that you're coming to a time of greater awareness or challenge. You might be preparing to go back to school or take on more responsibilities at work that require you to do a lot more logistical planning, and Sparrow may be a better help for that than Eagle. Or the new totem may tell you about changes that you may need to initiate in your life, lessons that you may not have known you needed to learn.

Again, keep in mind those primary, secondary, and tertiary categories of totems discussed in the first chapter.

Some totems do stay with us for life, but there's nothing wrong if some or even all of them come and go as they need to. Also, you may end up with multiple totems for one correspondence; in the previous example, Sparrow may come along and instead of replacing Eagle, may work in conjunction with her for a time.

Collecting Correspondences

Do you currently work with any sets of correspondences, such as those found in the tarot, runes, ogham, or other divination sets, astrology, Qabalah, alchemy, or other sets of symbols? Or do you have other personal associations you make?

For example, I associate certain times of the year with specific activities in my garden; spring is the time of planting the first seeds, while May and June are the time of strawberries. August and September are the one time a year I get fresh tomatoes, and late October is the only point when I have green tomato soup. These all have great spiritual significance to me, as I consider all the cycles of nature to be sacred. I mark these times throughout the year with occurrences that are unique to them.

I have not found specific animal totems for these times, though I do have plant totems for them. If you have similar personal correspondences like my garden times, you may consider working with animal totems you associate with them.

How to Use the Rest of this Chapter

While this chapter is going to discuss several different systems of correspondence that you can use as a structure for working with totems, the one I am going to present first and in the most detail is the directional system. This is partly because it can be a fairly simple system, especially if limited to the four cardinal directions, and it is also one I am personally quite familiar with.

I will be laying out a fairly complete introduction on how to work with the directional system. For the rest of the systems, I'll introduce what makes them unique and then explain how you can adapt some of the concepts and practices I discussed with the directional system to use with each of the others.

What happens if you feel that you can't connect with a particular part of a correspondence system? For example, I have met a number of people over the years who resonate with a particular element, but feel they can't connect to its "opposite." A "water person" may feel he or she simply cannot empathize with the element of fire at all, and so can't do any spiritual or magical work surrounding it. You may find that it helps to work with each element individually, or by remembering that our bodies are physically composed of all four of those elements and so we all have a direct, immediate connection to them. On the other hand, if you cannot or do not wish to work with a particular correspondence, don't feel pressured to force yourself just to have a "complete set," as it were. You may find you can connect better at a later point, or it may just be that you do better with that personal omission.

Justin has been working with the major arcana of the tarot for a while. He's had very deep spiritual experiences with most of them, but for some reason, any time the Wheel of Fortune card comes up, it never seems to fit into his readings. And when he meditates on the card's meanings, he can never really find any good parallels in his own life or experiences. The cyclical nature of it feels almost too neat in a world where spontaneity and even chaos can happen, and he keeps imagining the image of the Wheel of Fortune breaking and releasing the beings tied to it. Finally, he reaches a point where he decides to just leave the card out of the deck for his personal readings, and to stop trying to meditate on it. He feels that the rest of the cards create a better set of stories for him without it, and his readings and magical practice improve as a result.

The Directional System

One of the simplest systems connects totems to different directions—sometimes just the four cardinal directions, but others as well. Many cultures associate certain qualities with the directions, often based in the traveling of the sun and other celestial bodies across the sky, or by natural landmarks near where a community is based. It is also very common to associate the four cardinal directions with other "fours," such as the four classic Western elements (earth, air, fire, and water), or the four seasons.

So for example, since the sun comes up in the east, and spring is when life begins to reassert itself more visibly in the Northern Hemisphere, then east may equal spring. Air is the lightest and least encumbered element, so its breeziness can represent the easy-moving potential of new beginnings. South is summer and fire, as the sun is in the south and brings that southern heat with it, and the climate gets warmer the farther south one goes. West is fall, as the sun goes down and nature seems to go into decline, with trees losing leaves and animals migrating or preparing to hibernate; fall is also the rainy season for many areas, particularly temperate ones, and so water is often associated with west. And north can be seen as winter, when nature seems to be dormant; the farther north you go the colder it gets, and when the sun is gone at night everything cools down. As earth is the coldest and most solid, static element, the slowness and quiet of winter can also be connected with the element of earth.

Also, while my presentation of this system features the directions as the primary set of correspondences, with the elements and seasons and such as just some of the things associated with the directions, you may actually find that it's easier for you to connect to, for example, the elements rather than the directions themselves. If that's the case, just substitute the elements instead of the directions in all the exercises below—you might look for the totems associated with earth, air, fire, and water, or the Chinese elements of wood, fire, earth, metal, and water (perhaps rounding out the directions with a fifth, center).

This is just one potential example; different cultures have unique reasons for their own totem-direction pairings. There's no universal combination, and the directional totems vary according to geography and local fauna, cultural myths and associations, and other factors. And some cultures, to include my own nonindigenous American one, lack any directional totemic system at all, which sometimes means having to create those connections yourself.

My Own Experience

Way back when I first started discovering Neopaganism and, by extension, totemism, I hadn't quite grasped the usefulness of the Internet beyond chat rooms, and so I primarily looked to books for resources. And since I lived in a small town in a conservative area, there wasn't a Pagan shop within close range, either. Our library was of the sort that didn't have a lot of books on esoteric subject matter anyway, and much of what they had cataloged had mysteriously vanished at some point in the past, as such books are wont to do.

My main source of information was a small health food store that happened to carry a few books on alternative religions. Alongside some texts on Reiki, crystals, and other topics that appealed to a more general New Age audience, there was a limited selection of books on "Native American spirituality." Rarely was this ever discussed in terms of specific tribes, but rather in terms of "the Native American way," and generic "red road/black road" cosmologies. Some of it was presented by people of Native cultures, though I saw a good number of white writers who were purportedly taught by "Native elders" of varying dubiousness.

While even then I was suspicious of the generalities that were presented as genuine secrets of a whole slew of diverse cultures, I was trying to find some structure to my newfound spirituality and was not in a position to criticize—yet. When I found a few books on totemism and related topics to go alongside my copy of *Animal-Speak*, I gravitated toward the concept of the four directions and the various animals associated with them.

The animal/direction pairings I gravitated toward were as follows:

- North/Earth: Wolf

- East/Air: Eagle or Hawk

- South/Fire: Buffalo

- West/Water: Bear

The only animals I ever encountered in person in my area were red-tailed hawks. However, my longstanding relationship with Gray Wolf predated my discovery of Paganism by many years. And even before I started checking out these books, Brown Bear had started snuffling around my life. I saw many red-tailed hawks where I grew up, and so that made a good match for the sky. As for Buffalo? Well, I thought I may as well round everything out as suggested and give it a try.

At the time, it seemed to make sense. And so for many years I worked with these totems that I had adopted for the four directions, and it worked pretty well. Well enough, in fact, that when I tried changing all four of them to something that I thought should make more sense according to my more developed conception of what the directions stood for, my original four said, "Nope, we're staying."

Not that there was never any change, of course. And, most appropriately, it was in the south, the direction I associate with fire and transformation. Over the years, Buffalo stepped aside for Mustang, Cat, Coyote, and most recently Red Fox. Each of these moved into that place at a time in my life when they needed to be there, and although Buffalo has never regained that spot, I'm grateful for his time there.

Making Personal Connections

Even though my practice has wended its way through several types of practice, the one thing that has remained consistent has always been the directional totems. To this day, Gray Wolf, Brown Bear, and Red-tailed Hawk remain on my altar along with Red Fox, and I still greet them at the directions at the beginnings of rituals. I only ever see red-tailed hawks on a regular basis; I still have never seen a wolf or a bear in person other than at a zoo or wildlife sanctuary, and I've only seen wild foxes on a very small number of occasions, but the connection to the totems themselves remains strong.

I attribute this connection to the structure the directional system has given me based on the different correspondences associated with each direction. Correspondences are popular among Pagans simply because they offer a ready-made framework on which to base a practice, a way to bring together seemingly disparate magical and spiritual systems. However, I feel this has less to do with some universal mystical properties found in a set of beings/phenomena, and more with the human mind's tendency to look for and create patterns in the world around us. Bears, carrots, and quartz crystals all probably couldn't care less what element they're associated with or whether they could be worked into the symbolism of a tarot deck. In my experience, totems function as emissaries between our need for patterns and understanding, and a world that often doesn't make sense to us in its raw form. As mentioned earlier in the book, one way a totem can help us is by organizing and symbolizing the information and interpretation of that species in a way that makes our brains happy.

So Who Goes Where?

What does this mean in terms of a directional totemic system? Well, for one thing, it means that the animals that are "right" for each direction are not set in stone. Even among indigenous tribes that share similar wildlife and have animals associated with the directions, the animals will not necessarily be the same. Again, I don't feel it's so much some universal force that determines what tribe gets what animals, so much as it is the collective cultural psyche of the tribe that figures it out over time.

Most of you reading this book (including yours truly) are from more individualistic—as opposed to communal—cultures, and additionally cultures that don't have totemic systems in common use. You can see this as either a hindrance or an advantage.

On the one hand, there's something comforting about having a ready-made system to simply step into and adopt. Many of the answers people seek are already in place, mapped out neatly. Again, this is why correspondences are so popular and ubiquitous in magical writing. Plant A connects to Animal B, which is associated with Deity C, and so forth. Obviously, this is not the be-all and end-all of one's spirituality. Even the most extensive correspondences are just building blocks for more complex, personal experiences. But it can be nice to have those building blocks already laid out and ready to use, even with instructions.

However, simply adopting the totemism of another culture without being a part of that culture, if you lack your own, can be problematic. I've already discussed in detail the issue of cultural "neutrality." One of the hallmarks of "plastic shamanism" and other forms of cultural appropriation is that they very often try to yank elements of a culture's spirituality out of the context in which these elements were developed and then attempt to shoehorn them into another culture entirely. This is when we see (primarily white) American authors "borrowing" bits and pieces of Native American spiritualities and then squashing them into some hodgepodge of New Age and other non-Native spiritualities. While some of the concepts of various culture-specific spiritualities may be touted as "universal truths" and may indeed resemble each other at least superficially, cultural appropriation of spiritual "truths" is like uprooting a plant out of a wild place, sticking it in a pot in a room, and then calling the result a forest. You may have a plant in a place, but the context is very different in each case.

I tend to recommend to people in mainstream American and similarly nonanimistic cultures that rather than trying to co-opt someone else's totemism, create your own. Yes, this is a "do as I say, not as I did—sort of" situation. Had I been more aware of the cultural ramifications of starting my directional totemic work inspired by books that stemmed from rip-offs of Native cultural and spiritual practices, I probably would have gone about things differently. What I did worked for me, and I can't deny that. But at least I know enough to be able to say where my mistakes were and where I wish I might have acted differently.

Because Neopagan totemism is such an individualistic system anyway, you may as well take the opportunity to start forming some personal correspondences to work with, something that fits you better than prefabricated systems created by someone else at some other time and in some other context. The first thing you'll want to start with is the directions themselves.

What Do the Directions Mean to You?

The directions have always been there; ultimately, they're the way we orient ourselves in three-dimensional space. While there are specific places we have determined mark how far north or south we are (such as the poles), or how far east or west (longitude lines), there aren't physical directional markers not created by humans. Even then, terms like "north" and "south" are things we created to describe certain concepts of spatial orientation. We could just as easily turn all our globes and maps upside-down and consider "south" to be "up the map", and north to be "down under."

The fact remains that we are very visual and spatial creatures by nature; we place a lot of emphasis on our experience of being in a place. Therefore we can symbolically use the directions as ways to orient ourselves not only physically, but also emotionally, mentally, energetically, spiritually, etc. The totems of the directions are one form of embodiment of meaning attached to those directions, and they can help us by being a connection to greater concepts overall.

When I first committed myself to a specifically neo-shamanic path back in 2007, one of the things I did as a sort of spiritual "reboot" was to spend a month on each of the four cardinal directions, and then pulled what I learned into a coherent system, at least as much as I could at the time. I spent a month each working with earth, air, fire, and water, corresponding to north, east, south, and west respectively, determining what they meant to me, how they manifested in my life, and so forth. I would actively meditate with them, but I also had occurrences that happened in the world around me that added meaning to what I was doing. The entire exercise served to help me focus more clearly on what I had associated the directions and elements with over time, as well as developing some new meanings.

I already had the four totems I associated with them, so for me finding totems wasn't a goal. However, you can do a similar sort of intensive work over a period of time that includes not only correspondences with elements, directions and the like, but also finding the totems that will embody these things the most for you.

A quick side question: Why work with the totems of the directions instead of just the directions themselves? It is certainly possible to connect with the directions, or any other set of correspondences directly. However, I generally prefer to work with animal totems the most. They're easier for me to relate to than an element or a season, and I really just like working with animals a lot. I would guess that if you've picked up this book, you got it so you could learn to work with animal totems, too.

I'd like to make it clear that I'm not presenting a way to work with the directions through animal totems, in as much as this is a method of contacting animal totems using the directions as a structure for doing so. Many people have trouble with just saying, "Okay, I'm going to go find my totem!" because they don't feel they have a good place to start. But if they have some structure to work with—like "I want to find my totems of the north, east, south, and west!"—it helps narrow down what they're looking for and how they're going to find it.

You're certainly welcome to work with the directions themselves, and if this book happens to inspire you to venture into things that have little to nothing to do with totems, have fun exploring! This book's main purpose is to teach you different ways to get in touch with animal totems, so we'll stay focused on that.

If you want to start by acquainting yourself with the directions more fully, the following exercise is one way to try.

Inviting the Directions

Set aside a particular amount of time to work with each direction. I chose a month because it's a long enough period of time for things to happen, but not so long that I would lose attention. Find what amount of time you believe will work for you, though I wouldn't recommend anything shorter than a week because you'll want to have time to explore each direction and let it reveal more of itself to you. Some people may prefer to let the transitions from one direction to the next happen more organically instead of having a set time limit, letting the spirits and other powers that be give them cues as they go along.

Also, while I am primarily referring to the four cardinal directions in my own work, there's nothing stopping you if you want to include, say, the ordinals (northeast, southeast, southwest, northwest), center, up, down, and so forth. Just plan the time you'll need to work with each accordingly.

You may want to do a ritual to kick off your work before you even start working with the directions individually. I would suggest scheduling it a few days before you intend to start working with the first element. Here's one that may work for you; feel free to adjust it as you see fit:

What you'll need: Items that represent each of the directions, or a single compass; a drum, rattle, or other noisemaker, even your own two clapping hands; a space to set up an altar, small shrine, etc. for meditation; your notebook/journal and a pen/pencil.

A brief note on the representational items: these do not need to be expensive or flashy. Some of my favorite items for the directions on my altar are small stones, sticks, pine cones, etc. from special places I've hiked, arranged according to where they are in relation to my home. You can also simply use cards with the names of the directions written on them, embellished if you like.

Preparation: Set up the altar or shrine in a place where it won't be in the way but where you have a little space to meditate in front of it or at least see it daily. If you can't keep it assembled at all times, have a safe place to keep the components, and try to keep it simple so that setting it up and breaking it down doesn't take long. Put the directional symbols in their appointed places; or, if you have a compass, place it so the "N" is facing north, in the center of the altar/shrine.

Sit or stand before the altar/shrine, wherever you wish to begin. I prefer north myself, but it's entirely up to you. State the following in a clear voice:

Spirits of the Directions, of
[name all the directions you wish to work with],
It is time for me to set foot upon a new path.
Though I have lived my
entire life surrounded by you,
I wish to know you more deeply.
So I dedicate to each of you a [period of time you
will work with each, such as a week or month]
so that I may more fully understand
who you are in my world.
In the same way I offer myself to you
as a listening ear and learning mind,
I invite you, Spirits of the Directions.
Join me in this endeavor.
Help me to know your place here!
North! East! South! West!
[Or whatever directions you call on]
Let this place be open to you!

Once the invocation is done, sit down in a comfortable place by the altar/shrine with your journal and pen, and write what you observe. Give yourself at least fifteen to twenty minutes to allow the spirits to communicate with you. Remember that not all communication from spirits is obvious nor verbal.

When you are ready to complete the ritual, put your hands on the altar and say,

Spirits of the Directions,
[names of all the directions you wish to work with],
I have made my invitation; let this
small place in my home be your home as well.
Let it be a haven here for you
and a reminder of you for me.
Let it be our place to connect together.
Spirits of the Directions, welcome home!

Once you are done, either leave the altar where it will live permanently, or put the components in a safe place. The spirits will know where it is regardless. Write down any other impressions or thoughts you have.

Give yourself a few days to let this ritual "percolate," as it were. In the time between this ritual and starting with your first element, pay attention to anything that reminds you of the elements or causes you to feel their presence more strongly. Again, the directions are always there; it is our perception and understanding of their meaning to us that can change.

Working with Individual Directions

The information in this section can be applied to any direction; simply adjust names and details as needed. Again, you're welcome to personalize what's here; this is just to get you started.

One way to get started is to speak with the spirit of the direction. This is the embodiment of the direction itself, not the totem associated with it. If I were doing this sort of ritual, I would be working directly with north itself instead of working with Gray Wolf, my animal totem of the north.

As with the general evocation of all the directions, you may also wish to start each direction's time period with a ritual for it. You can write a ritual for each individual direction or you may also use this or another general one:

Sit or stand before the altar/shrine, holding the item associated with the spirit of the direction with which you wish to work. You may also make a small offering to the spirit; this can be a piece of artwork or writing, another small item that reminds you of the direction, etc.

Invite the spirit to work with you. Use your own words or this invocation, if you like:

> *Spirit of [Direction],*
> *You have made your home here with me.*
> *I now invite you to join me for the next*
> *[period of time].*
> *Here is what I know of you:*
> *[tell the spirit as much as you know about it].*
> *I ask you to help me know more and to know what*
> *you most wish me to understand about you.*
> *I will give you my attention and awareness, and do*
> *my best to honor what you offer me.*
> *Join me now, if you will, Spirit of [Direction]!*

Again, write down any immediate impressions you have. Then spend the time you have allotted for working with the spirit, whether a week or month or other, paying attention to anything you associate with that direction, doing research, and seeing what stands out to you the most, or to what the spirit tells you to pay special attention.

It's also a good idea to meditate regularly with the spirit of that direction. You may wish to do this at your altar/shrine, but any place where you can face or otherwise be immersed in the direction will work. Incorporating things you associate with the direction also can be helpful. For example, if you're working with east and associate it with air, try meditating facing east on a hilltop on a breezy day.

Over the time period, a totem may step forward as a representative of that direction. It's possible you'll make it through the time period allotted and not ever get a hint of a single creature; conversely, you may feel too many are appearing and that you're unable to determine which one deserves the most attention.

If either of these is the case for you, try doing a guided meditation specifically to meet with the totem of the direction. You can use the meditation provided in Appendix B. Before you start, make sure you are facing the direction whose totem you are seeking, and go into the meditation with the intent of finding that totem specifically. Part of the meditation involves going through a tunnel and coming out into a natural place to meet the totem; when you get to that place in the meditation, you can even call out for the totem, something like: *"Totem of the [Direction], I seek your guidance, and I request your presence in joining me in this place!"* or whatever feels most appropriate in the moment.

If this still doesn't work, ask the spirit of the direction whether you should spend more time with it or simply move on and allow the totem to appear at its own pace. You may find that you don't have a single totem show up until you've worked your way all the way through all the directions you've chosen to work with, and then they may all appear at once at the end!

Finally, it is possible for someone to have more than one totem for a given direction. Depending on the situation, they may both want to work together or take turns holding that energy. Using guided meditation, talk with them and ask them how they would prefer to work.

One other note specifically regarding correspondences: even after you've completed the quest for your directional totems, you may find that you continue to create connections between the totems and other things, such as colors or natural phenomena, or purposes like healing or dreamwork. Keep recording everything, and over time you may develop your own personal library of correspondences that has a lot more power to it than generalized, "popular" sets of correspondences. Even if yours go against what others say, keep it up if it's working for you!

Further Work with Directional Totems

Once you have determined who your directional totems are, there are a number of ways you can incorporate them into your practice.

Greeting the Directions

The simplest is through calling on the totems whenever you greet the directions, whether in a circle casting, another creation of sacred space, or any time you feel the need for the protection and stability of grounding yourself.

You may also call on the totems instead of (or in addition to) any other spiritual beings you associate with the directions, such as the watchtowers or the four winds. Sometimes this may be as simple as swapping out names in the ritualistic words you already use. However, you can also create invocations specifically for the totems. The one that I've used throughout my work with directional totems has been the following:

> *Great [insert totem's name here] of the [direction],*
> *I greet thee and I ask thee to watch*
> *over me this day/night.*

After I say this invocation, I give the totem a few moments to "arrive." Often I will feel the totem throughout my body, a sort of very brief shapeshifting, as it uses my body and mind as a conduit to enter my sacred space. You may not have this experience, or you may seem to hear the rush of wings or smell musky fur as the totem settles into its appointed quarter.

When my ritual is done, I say farewell with the following:

> *Great [insert totem's name here] of the [direction],*
> *I thank thee for watching over me this day/night.*
> *Go if you must, stay if you will,*
> *but remember me always,*
> *for you are a part of me, and I am a part of you.*

You don't have to use the same invocation format for every one of the directional totems. Each one may want something specific to them. For example, for Gray Wolf I might say:

> *Great Gray Wolf of the North Wind,*
> *shaggy-furred and watchful,*
> *keeper of pack and pups,*
> *hunter and scavenger both,*
> *howling across the plains,*
> *forests, and mountains,*
> *join me now in this sacred place.*

For Red-tailed Hawk, I could offer:

> *Great Red Hawk of the East Wind,*
> *your wings are outstretched above me.*
> *I hear your keening cry,*

and I pray I catch your eye.
I offer you a place to rest a while here.

You might even try saying something different, speaking from your heart each time. The words aren't important so much as the connection. If you can create a space for the totems to be in during your ritual/meditation/etc., the effectiveness is most important. And if you've never done this before, give yourself some patience. It takes practice to find the words and perform the rite itself. Try out different things and see what works best for you over time.

Spellwork and Other Magic

Correspondences are good for more than just being able to identify connections between totems, elements, and other concepts. They can also be used in more active magical and spiritual work.

Many spells call for components that follow certain correspondences; for example, there are stones commonly associated with healing, herbs associated with protection, etc. When possible, refer to your own personalized correspondences; "universal" ones may also be applicable depending on the situation.

Let's say you want to do a spell to promote a friend's speedy recovery from a minor illness such as a cold. You associated west with water and healing, and your totem of the west is Common Starfish (whose children are the chunky, bumpy, five-armed, bright orange starfish many people in the Northern Hemisphere are familiar with). You want to do a candle-burning spell, so you get a candle of a color you associate with healing—let's say blue in this case. You put it in the west portion of your altar or other working space and surround it with stones, herbs, or other items that also have a healing energy for you.

But where to put Starfish? You might carve a starfish into the candle, or put a small picture or other replica of one next to the candle holder. Then ask Starfish for help with the healing; for example, you could say:

> *Ancient star, mirroring the sky in the waters below*
> *I ask for your help, let your energy flow!*
> *Healing waters surround you and cradle you well,*
> *salt in water, let this illness quickly quell!*

A directional totem may also have ideas on how to create a spell or ritual for a particular need whether you had previous plans or not. In my experience, it has generally been beneficial to listen well to what the totems have to say, especially since they are taking the time to help you out. They can often provide perspectives you might not have considered.

This type of help and advice can also happen in complex rituals too. The structure you use may be different and the intents may be weightier, but the concept is the same—you're asking the totems for help and protection while you make the magic happen. Here are the important things to remember:

- Use the personalized correspondences you've developed while getting to know the totems as much as possible; this serves as a sort of shared language.

- Play to the totems' strengths *as they present them to you*. Although Whitetail Deer is sometimes associated with psychic abilities, don't assume that that's what Deer would help you with, especially if Deer has indicated wanting to help you with, say, exercise and getting outside more. Something that someone else reports as a "power" of a totem may not be the case universally, or the totem may simply wish to work with you on something different and not become distracted.

- Combine your ideas with those of the totems, and actively invite the totems to participate when the time comes to do the work.

- Offerings are a great idea before or after you work your magic.

Map versus Territory

A very important thing to keep in mind: the map is not the territory. While you are creating your own personal cosmology based on the directions and what you associate with them, remember that this cosmology is a representation of the physical world (and in some cases, the universe).

Physically speaking, the directions are simply where everything is in relation to a particular point, such as the place where you are at a given time. Most of the properties we assign to the directions are subjective meanings we or other people create. Sometimes these associations seem pretty arbitrary.

A good example is the correspondences between the cardinal directions (north, south, east, west) and the four classic elements (earth, air, fire, water). Many Neopagans and others associate north with earth, west with water, east with air (or, according to some, fire), and south with fire (or air, depending).

For the most part, these are primarily passed on through various ceremonial traditions, not grounded in any physical place a person may live. I do know of a few people who deliberately changed things around to match their bioregion—for example, if there is a large body of water to the east, that direction might then match up more naturally with water as an element. On the other hand, it's not always that simple. Here in northeast Portland, I have the Columbia River to the north, the Willamette River (and farther out, the Pacific Ocean) to the west, and the Bull Run watershed (where my drinking water comes from) to the east, as well as the Johnson Creek watershed to the south. Really, there's water everywhere I go!

In a way, most of us aren't working with physical directions and elements as much as abstractions thereof.

This is not necessarily a mistake—we are meaning-making creatures. A set of correspondences tells a story, and provides a framework we can use to better understand different concepts. We can associate the four seasons with directions—spring in the east, summer in the south, and so forth, and use the correspondences thereof to enhance our seasonal rituals. If we feel surrounded by a particular element in all physical directions, such as being on an island surrounded by water, having a model based on abstracts can help us determine which element goes with which direction.

I don't believe we should only base our knowledge of totems on preexisting totem dictionaries, nor do I believe that we should ignore the place of our own created cosmologies in light of the physical place we live. That goes for the directional totems, too.

In my own case, only two of the four animals I associate with directions may be commonly found in my part of Oregon—red-tailed hawks and red foxes. There is a small number of gray wolves reported in the northeastern part of the state, and there are bears here and there, though they're black bears, not brown. This isn't as extreme as if I had African Lion and Kiwi as two of my directional totems. But if I were to start all over from scratch and find new directional totems, or at least a second set that are specific to this area, I might end up with more local common totems, like Scrub Jay or Nutria.

If you feel the need to really ground yourself in the place you live, be aware of the major physical landmarks in your area, maybe within a fifty-mile radius as a start. If there are certain ones that stand out—say, a mountain in the south, which could be earth—use those as the basis of your directional correspondence work, as opposed to just going with north = earth, if it makes more sense for you. Additionally, you can include the intent in your initial ritual when you first greet the directions for which you would like to find local totems to work with; say it out loud just to make it clear. (If you find this sort of local grounding really important, you may like the Bioregional Model discussed in the next chapter.)

Other Systems of Correspondence

I've gone into a lot of depth about the directional system as an illustration of one way that you can use the Correspondences Model of totemism in this chapter. You can use any system of correspondences you see fit; following are a few examples.

Zodiac (Chinese)

This one seems almost too simple at first glance. Each of the twelve signs of this zodiac is represented by an animal: Rat, Ox, Tiger, Rabbit, Dragon, Snake, Horse, Goat, Monkey, Rooster, Dog, and Pig. Each one of these is associated with one year in a twelve-year cycle, a month-long period throughout the year, certain days throughout the year, and a particular time of each day. Not every Rat year is the same, either; one Rat year may be associated with metal; the next one, twelve years later, is the year of the Water Rat, and twelve years after that is the Wood Rat, and so forth. Each sign also has a very distinctive set of positive and negative personality traits associated with it that resembles the behaviors of the animals themselves. According to this system, you can figure out whether someone else is a good relationship prospect depending on when you both were born.

Yet, it's what you do with the information that makes it more than just a simple set of correspondences. For starters, you can take the time to get to know each of the twelve animals (which, for the purposes of our work here, we will include under the category of "totem," although it is not exactly their original function in Chinese astrology). Your birth year may be associated with just one of them, but every day is touched by all of them at some point. They may all have lessons to teach through their strengths…and weaknesses.

Additionally, they may also work with or even introduce you to other totems not in their original system, but which have similar qualities. I was born in the year of the Earth Horse, and Mustang did ground me during my difficult teenaged years, working in tandem with my primary totem, Gray Wolf. Again, the basic Chinese astrology system may be a starting point that helps you expand into work with other totems.[12]

The Western Zodiac and Related Correspondences

This astrological system also features twelve main signs; however, only some of them are directly represented by animals. There's Scorpio(n), Taurus the bull, Aries the ram, Cancer the crab, Leo the lion, Pisces the fish, as well as Capricorn the fish-goat hybrid, and Sagittarius the half-horse centaur. But what of Aquarius, Gemini, Virgo, and Libra, three human signs and an object?

There are numerous tables of correspondences in Western magical and mystery traditions, including some that involve real and fantastic animals. Looking at my copy of Aleister Crowley's *777*, a classic book of correspondences, I can see that the twelve Western zodiac signs listed in Column VI of Table I correspond to twelve numbers between fifteen and twenty-nine. (Three of those numbers, oddly enough, are represented by the planets Jupiter and Mars and the element of water.) Those same numbers

---

12. While I've been referring to Chinese astrology in this section, it's more properly "the American idea of what Chinese astrology is." Similarly to other indigenous systems, care should be taken when exploring Chinese astrology outside its original cultural context. Rather than reiterate the last chapter's material on cultural appropriation *ad infinitum*, I will simply recommend applying the same judgment and caution to the use of all other culture-specific systems mentioned in this chapter.

each correspond to a specific animal or animals over in Table I, Column XXXVIII. For example, Taurus is associated with the number sixteen in these tables, and the animal associated with that number is, appropriately, the bull. However, Libra is twenty-two, and the corresponding animal is the elephant. This might reflect Elephant's calm and deliberate movements that we may interpret as "balance," for example.

It may sound a bit confusing, and to be sure Crowley managed to fit a lot of information in his tables; if you aren't familiar with his writing and organizational style, it may take a bit of getting used to. However, there are numerous other newer books of correspondences that may be more accessible. Bill Whitcomb's *The Magician's Companion* is one possible resource; it's a well-received and very thorough example that links together elements of various cultural and spiritual traditions in an easy-to-follow manner.

As you're searching through the many tables of correspondences, you may find many references to the Qabalah (alternately spelled Kabbalah or Cabala). This is a form of Jewish mysticism based on the Tree of Life, a set of ten spheres (Sephiroth) and twenty-two paths between them, which may be ascended through ceremony and meditation to achieve oneness with the divine. The rich complexity of Qabalistic symbolism is at the heart of much of Western, particularly European, mystical symbolism, and links between the animals of Crowley's 777 and various elements of Qabalah may also be found through research.

One of the best-known portrayals of Qabalistic and related symbolism is the tarot, one of a number of divination systems from around the world. Let's look more into those, shall we?

Tarot, Runes, and Other Divination Symbol Systems

A divination system is a set of symbols used to predict future events, or otherwise divine information about a situation that may not be accessible through "normal" means. Some consider divination to be a matter of psychic abilities, while others attribute it to the natural intuitive powers of the human mind. There are also those who use divination tools to ask spirits for answers.

Cultures worldwide have created a variety of divination systems. Of Italian origin, the tarot is full of complex symbolism that stems from older playing cards (which may also be used for divination). Simpler, but not less powerful, sets of symbols may be found in Norse, Anglo-Saxon, and Icelandic runes, while several Celtic cultures used similar systems known as ogham. Farther east, the Chinese created the I Ching, and one of many African cultures' divination systems is the Yoruban Ifá.

Many of these have at least some animal symbolism associated with them. In the Norse Elder Futhark of runes, the rune Uruz represents the (now sadly extinct) aurochs, a type of wild cattle, while Fehu stands for its domestic counterpart, the cow. Ehwaz is the horse, while Algiz is "elk"—what we in North America know as the moose.

Some of these systems are quite animal-centric; the Celtic ogham provides a good example. The origin of the ogham may be found in the names of each of the symbols, or *feda* (singular *fid*), which may mean things like the beauty of women, an iron bar, or a young plant, but these word oghams are just the beginning. There are oghams (or sets of meanings associated with the *feda*) for all sorts of things and concepts. The best-known may be the tree ogham popularized by Robert Graves, but there are oghams for colors, musical notes—and birds.

The bird ogham connects different species of bird to each of the *feda*. Dair, the *fid* meaning "oak tree," also corresponds to the wren. Tinne, or "bar of metal," is associated with the starling, and so forth. While the bird ogham is one of the traditional oghams used by the Celts themselves, there doesn't seem to have been one for a more general collection of animals.[13] Several authors and other practitioners of Celtic spirituality have created their own animal oghams based on Celtic mythology and animals important to those cultures. One good example is John

---

13. Erynn Rowan Laurie, *Ogam: Weaving Word Wisdom* (Stafford, UK: Megalithica Books, 2007).

Michael Greer's animal ogham, which connects animals like the mouse, hedgehog, and badger to various *feda*.[14]

Pantheons of Deities

Some may take offense at the idea of deities themselves being symbols, but as they embody natural phenomena, human ideals and traits, and other qualities, they may be considered symbolic in that way.

Deities in pantheons across the world are associated with animals, sometimes very closely. Most of the dynastic Egyptian deities are portrayed with animal heads—Anubis the Jackal, Bast the Cat, Horus the Hawk, and so on. The Greek gods and Roman deities who were derived from them also have strong animal connections. The peacock is sacred to Hera/Juno, while Artemis/Diana favors hounds, deer, and bears, among other wildlife. Freya's white cats and Odin's wolves and ravens are just a few examples of animals sacred to Norse deities. And many Hindu deities are portrayed as animals or as riding animals; Ganesha has the head of an elephant, and his steed is a rat.

Animals associated with deities are not automatically totemic in the traditional, kinship-related manner of the concept; the jackal of Anubis is not necessarily analogous to the totem Wolf of some Native American Plains cultures. Animals associated with deities are often seen as

---

14. John Michael Greer, *The Druidry Handbook: Spiritual Practice Rooted in the Living Earth* (York Beach, ME: Weiser Books, 2006).

emanations or bailiwicks (metaphorical spheres of authority) of that deity, and do not always stem from earlier, true totemisms based in human kinship and group identification. Also, even within the same culture there may be different beings "inspired by" the same animal species. Coyote the trickster god of several indigenous American cultures shares some qualities with Coyote the totem, but the god is more anthropomorphic and wrapped in a specific series of legends and myths. So saying that Coyote the god is the same as Coyote the totem is like equating Anubis and Jackal.

That being said, we may work with the totems of animals associated with deities of a particular pantheon. If a totem is partly "made of" all the lore surrounding an animal, then that includes the mythos related to deities. The totem may draw from the deity's lore and experiences and embody some similar qualities.

How to Use Other Systems

Now that I've given you some more potential systems to work with, here's how you apply them to the Correspondences Model. The basic methods can be summed up as follows:

- Identify the system that you would like to work with. This includes knowing at least the most basic correspondences (such as the four directions and the elements associated with them, the seventy-eight cards of the tarot, the twenty-four Elder Futhark runes, or the ten Sephiroth of the Qabalah).

• Introduce yourself to the spirits of the correspondences to familiarize yourself with them and the structure they represent. Let them know what you're trying to accomplish (finding the animal totems associated with them).

• Seek out the totems associated with each of the correspondences. For a more complex system like the tarot, you may look for just the totems of larger, overarching categories, such as the major arcana and the four suits of the minor arcana. Or you may choose to find the totem for each of the seventy-eight cards.

• Work with the totems to see how they fit into your life and spirituality. See if you connect to some better than others, and find out if there are reasons for it. Look at the other qualities associated with the totems you are more comfortable with, such as personality traits, magical or spiritual bailiwicks, elements, and other symbols or concepts they may embody. Why do those attract you more? What qualities do the totems you're less attached to or comfortable with have, and how do you feel about them?

· Integrate what you've learned about these totems into more practical work. If you want to change a habit you have, for example, is there a totem who may be a good fit for helping you? Is there a totem who has a specific thing they want to pass on to you? Are there totems who can help you with things like protecting your home, improving your health, or teaching you more about the world around you? Are there totems asking *you* for help?

When working with any sort of system in the Correspondences Model, you may find that multiple correspondences come into play. We've already seen that with the directional system, but here's just one of many ways that could happen within another system:

Sharon is interested in working with the birds associated with the Celtic ogham. Her first step is to find out which fid *(symbol) each bird is associated with and the basic meaning and qualities of that* fid. *Then she would want to get to know the totems of these species of birds to see what else they can tell her besides the information she's already found through her research. She decides to start with Ailm, the* fid *associated with the lapwing. Since there are several species of lapwing, she chooses to work with the totems of more than one of them, starting with Northern Lapwing.*

Using the totemic guided meditation in Appendix B, Sharon goes to meet Northern Lapwing for the first time. She wears a necklace with an image of Ailm on it while she meditates to help strengthen the connection. When she first meets Northern Lapwing, he is sitting in a pine tree, the tree of Ailm. Sharon shows Lapwing her necklace, and sings a note at the E below middle C, Ailm's note.

Lapwing is pleased, and greets Sharon. He sings to her in return, and in that song there is the sound of change, the gates of birth and of death. He tells her it is quite appropriate that she started her journey with him, as it is a new beginning for her, and Ailm is the fid *of thresholds.*

Over time and many visits, Lapwing and Sharon use the symbolism surrounding Ailm to help her establish a foundation upon which she may work with the bird totems of the other ogham feda. *Lapwing also introduces her to Eurasian Brown Bear, the representative of Ailm in one animal ogham. Bear's children have long been extinct in the areas where the Celts traditionally lived, and so Bear is able to tell Sharon more about the death transition of Ailm.*

Again, the example of systems of correspondence and the exercises presented are just a few of the options you have in working with the Correspondences Model of animal totemism. Any system of correspondences should work for mapping out a grouping of animal totems to meet and work with; find one that makes a good starting point for you.

A final reminder: while there are many historical and well-established correspondences, don't be afraid if your own observations differ from them. For example, if you're working with a zodiac, and the animal associated with a particular month turns out to be different for you (for example, Peacock for Scorpio/November instead of the Scorpion), explore that and see if it's a better connection for you. You may find that, over time, Peacock fits your understanding of the symbolism of November better than Scorpion.

Or you might be working with the ogham, and decide to create your own animal ogham based on what you know of each of the *feda* and the animals you feel most resemble their energies. Some of those animals may have had nothing to do with any Celtic culture, but in your experience they feel right.

Ultimately, correspondences are about multiple levels of symbolism used to better understand the world and the patterns in it. Therefore, it's better to adopt symbols that resonate with you, even if they aren't historically "correct." As long as you aren't claiming that your new system is something ancient, and the system works for you, then go with it!

Four

The Bioregional
Model of Totemism

In more than a decade of studying totemism, working with totems, and talking to people about their totems, I've noticed a peculiar phenomenon. Many people rarely, if ever, see the physical counterparts of the totems they work with, and very often this is because they don't live in the same place. Additionally, the tendency of people to gravitate toward the Big, Impressive North American Birds and Mammals tips the odds in favor of wild creatures that live in remote locations away from most people.

If this describes your totem, it doesn't mean you're doing it wrong. There are a lot of benefits to a more global approach to totemism, such as being able to connect with a wider variety of animals. On the other hand, it's also valuable to consider that indigenous totems have helped people to connect with the animals in their own area, an experience nonindigenous people often miss out on. This form of totemism, known as bioregional totemism, can be woven into a broader understanding of place.

What Is Bioregionalism?

Bioregionalism is one way people are trying to reclaim a closer connection to the land they live on. Instead of looking at arbitrary human boundaries such as state or country lines, a place is defined by natural phenomena such as waterways and geographic formations. For example, instead of saying that I am from Portland, Oregon, I might instead say I live in the Bull Run watershed in the Willamette Valley ecoregion, a part of Cascadia. This identifies the nearest river and what feeds it, the valley surrounding the Willamette River, and then the very large bioregion of Cascadia, which overlaps much of the Pacific Northwest. Each of these places are further made distinct from surrounding places by their unique flora and fauna (native and nonnative alike), as well as geological makeup and microclimate. To put it simply, you'll know a place by its animals and plants, as well as what the land, weather, and seasons are like.

Notice that so far I've been focusing mostly on bioregionalism's environmental elements. While connecting with the land, plants, and animals comprises the premiere element of bioregionalism, it also invites you to explore your relationships with the cultures and other human elements in your home region. Classic bioregionalism also entails other social and political ideals apart from environmentalism, such as feminism and other civil rights, communal living, locavorism (eating food grown within a short distance from home), and so forth. I leave it up to you to determine how much of this to incorporate into your personal vision of bioregionalism. Above all, the focus of bioregionalism is to bring us into greater connection with what we're a part of.

This opens up a crucial point in this chapter: humans are a part of the land, no matter how much we have altered it for our own uses. When we think of "nature," we very often evoke pictures of beautiful scenery, animals, plants, and so forth—and nary a human to be found other than the beholder. While this may appear to be a way to protect nature by removing us and our harmful influences, in fact it is counterproductive to environmental protection. The key problem is that we have perceived ourselves as being increasingly distant from the natural world, though historically it's been mainly due either to delusions of superiority, or distractions of our own making that take our focus away from the physical world around us.

Thinking of humans and our creations as "unnatural" is another way of creating that artificial distance. We are animals, and our cities and other creations are the result of the big brains and opposable thumbs we evolved over time. The harm we cause does not remove us from the cycles we are affecting. When we think of humans as blights upon the earth and try to separate ourselves from everyone else as the exception to the rule, not only are we abandoning the rest of nature to continued damage, we are also abandoning our fellow humans and giving up on any hope of changing the way things are.

Bioregionalism may at first seem to be yet another way to "purify" nature of human taint, but look again: humans and our cultures are seen as integral to the places we live in. Bioregionalism doesn't tell us to abandon civilization; rather, it encourages us to rethink our boundaries (physical and otherwise), and to more fully immerse ourselves in the places we live to the point where we can't ignore the problems we've created. It is a participatory movement, one that encourages us to be inclusive rather than exclusive. If anything, it is the people who perceive themselves as the most detached from nature who need to be engaged, not abandoned.

Soapbox aside, bioregionalism can be accessed by anyone, anywhere, because everyone is in a bioregion, even in the middle of a city. We're not generally taught how to identify the bioregion, however. Other than some vague explanations of things like what makes a desert a desert, geography classes generally look mostly at human boundaries and phenomena. If you have some catching up to do, don't feel bad—outside of a relatively few scientists and naturalists, most of us are in the same boat. And now's as good a time as any to redirect where we're sailing!

Getting Oriented (or Occidentaled!) to Your Bioregion

I have it easy in that bioregionalism had its birth in the Pacific Northwest where I live, and so there's been a lot of work identifying what the bioregions here are like, where they begin and end, and what to call the place I live. If you don't have this information provided for you already, there may be a permaculture or other environmental group in your area, some of whose members may be familiar with bioregionalism, or may find the concept intriguing enough to explore with you. There are also numerous websites available on the topic and a growing collection of relevant books, some of which may be found in my bibliography.

Let's say you're entirely on your own, though, with limited resources. The first thing you want to do is to identify your bioregion in general. An alternate term for bioregion is *ecoregion* so you may have better luck using that term. For example, the U.S. Environmental Protection Agency refers to several levels of ecoregion in the United States. If you've done much traveling in your area, you may have discovered that there are distinct changes in the land as you travel farther from home. Compare your experiences to a map of ecoregions so you have both the firsthand, up-close-and-personal perspective, as well as the broader bird's-eye view offered by the map and the research behind it.[15]

As mentioned earlier, I am in the Willamette Valley ecoregion as determined by the EPA. The ecoregion is physically marked by the Willamette River, its watershed, and the valley in which it flows. While all the phenomena in a bioregion are important, the watershed and waterways are probably most important. Not only is water one of the most important shapers of the land, but its location and availability are among the primary driving factors in the evolution of the plants and animals nearby. This includes the entire water cycle: from precipitation to surface and ground waters, to evaporation, and all over again. Water is the underlying base coat of paint on the canvas of the land; everything else is details added to this foundation.

---

15. The EPA has a good overview of North American ecoregions at http://www.epa.gov/wed/pages/ecoregions.htm. Searching for "lists of ecoregions by country" on Wikipedia reveals a surprisingly thorough list of world ecoregions.

A desert is a very good example. I once spent a few days in Arizona near Sedona during a lovely period in spring. Much of this dry land was shaped by wind erosion, though I hiked along dry washes that must have filled to the brim with periodic rains. The day was hot, though it was only in the eighties, so I saw very few animals besides myself. I knew they were resting in shady places out of the sun, preparing for the cooler evening. Doing so allowed them to conserve hydration.

The animals' bodies must also have been tailored for less use of water, and this practice was mirrored by the abundant plant life I met. As I picked my way through stands of juniper and yucca, I marveled at how these flora were able to survive in such a dry place. Their physical textures were themselves dry to the touch, with none of the lushness found in my more familiar ferns and maples. The tallest trees were just over thirty feet high with the exception of a few grand old cottonwoods right at a stream's edge.

People mirrored this scarcity of water, too. As I would come and go from Sedona proper, I marveled at how quick the transition from town to open desert was, with very few settlements in the latter. Although I had seen the gigantic sprawl of Phoenix on my flight's descent, Sedona was my home base during my visit. I grew up in the Midwest, where farmland is being chewed up by cheap suburban housing at an alarming rate, and I realized that growth was allowable primarily due to the abundance of water. Here, the ability of a town or city to expand was limited by water supplies—or at least it should have been. The presence of golf courses and green lawns in the desert belied the fragility of the water supplies there.

Contrast all that with my current home in the Pacific Northwest—or, as we joke, North*wet*. Where Sedona gets less than twenty inches of precipitation a year, Portland gets close to forty. The ground around Portland is much more absorbent, while the lower average temperatures also help the retention of water. Our primary source of potable water is the Bull Run watershed, fed by drainage from Mount Hood and surrounding elevations. We have nearly an embarrassment of riches when it comes to fresh water.

Over time, the rivers and streams that sluice through the area have carved up the land, wearing away stones formed through geologic upheaval and volcanic activity. The soil is very rich in places, fed not only by waterways but a diversity of plants that preserve the nutrients in each place generation after generation.

When I'm hiking in the Columbia River Gorge, I see many animals even in the middle of the day. Most of these are birds like juncos and ravens, along with countless insects, but I've also spotted elk, shrews, snakes, and others who venture out into the sun or rain. A midday stroll is not a death sentence, at least not from heat stroke. Most of these animals require more water to survive than their desert counterparts, and often need to drink directly from waterways rather than getting their hydration mainly from their food, whether other animals or plants.

If anything speaks to the watery paradise that is this area, it is the plant life. Whether you're in a forest, a floodplain, or the banks of a stream, the number of species of plant—as well as the sheer volume of individuals—can be overwhelming! One square foot of forest floor may contain a dozen or more plant species, from tiny fir seedlings to moss to multiple types of fern. The generous amount of water means that plants here tend to compete more for sunlight, sap-rich stems and trunks feeding a race to the top.

As you've been reading this, notice how everything comes back to the water. This is why waterways are so crucial in identifying and getting to know a bioregion. The way everything else living develops, and even the formation of land itself to a great extent, depends on the amount and nature of the water.

If you're going to get to know your bioregion face to face, start with the waterways—running waters like rivers and streams are the most dynamic; however, lakes and ponds indicate movement as well, as they are fed by watersheds, and often may be the beginning or end of streams themselves. Springs are important too, especially as they may contain some of the cleanest water in your area. And if you live near a sea or ocean, there's no ignoring the effect it has on the place you live.

Pick a waterway and get to know it and the land around it. How long has this waterway been here? Is it an ancient river that has carved a canyon a hundred feet deep into the surrounding rock? Is it a human-made pond originally designed for watering livestock? How much water is there, and how clean is it? Where's the next nearest source of water? Where is it all coming from? Directly from the sky, or also from higher regions, flowing downhill? How much demand is there for it as a resource? How do the climate and the seasonal weather affect the presence or lack of water?

Next, familiarize yourself with the plants and animals that live nearby. (Yes, it's okay if you need to consult a field guide for identification.) What is their relationship to the water, and how much competition is there for it? How deep are the roots of the plants, and how far must they go to hit groundwater, if any? Do the animals drink the water directly? Do they bathe in it? Spawn in it? Live in or on it?

And yes, since we are talking about animal totems in particular, pay close attention to whom you find there. Don't just pull the animals out of context, though. You've spent this much time getting to know their environment—understand them as they are within it. Notice which plants the animal or its prey feeds on. Pay attention to how often it visits the water, and why. Note where in the land it likes to be, whether underground or on top of high plateaus, hidden, out in the open, or in the sky above. What is this animal's niche?

Now we start getting into the roots of bioregional animal totemism. Before we move on, though, a few notes about the *human* animal…

We Are Still of the Land

I want to reiterate the idea that we are ourselves animals, and no matter how urbanized we are, we are still of the land. No exploration of any bioregion would be complete without taking our own species into account. Perhaps even more importantly, we need to be aware of how much we have changed the bioregion through cities and other human development. The reduction in wilderness and the increase in everything from agricultural land to fields of skyscrapers have wrought great changes. The land looks different; the water may have been redirected and its ability to support life diminished; some species of animals and plants may have left or even gone extinct, while others may have gone into overdrive to fill empty niches. And on a greater scale, the effects of global climate change have been unfolding more dramatically in recent decades.

It does no good to look only at the nonhuman parts of a bioregion, especially one heavily altered by human activity. A bioregion doesn't stop where the pavement ends. It changes, but it still exists as an ecosystem, albeit one perhaps very different from its previous incarnations.

Since so many of you live in cities and towns, many of your experiences with the land will be with a more tamed, cultivated, even paved-over place.

Living in an urban environment is not a cause for shame. You are not a bad person just for living in a city, nor are you less spiritual than someone who lives in an intentional community miles away from the nearest paved road. If anything, it is crucial to identify the bioregional markers in urban areas because it can make the concept of bioregionalism more accessible to someone who is unable or unwilling to go out into the wilderness.

Let us also consider a bioregion's human inhabitants, be it in the wilderness, deep in the city, or somewhere in between. Think about where the water runs through. Where did that water come from, and where does it go? What human habitations does it touch? How do the people respond to the water? Is the use of the water responsible or wasteful? Has the flow of the water been changed by people, whether through rerouting streams, damming rivers, paving, or excessive water consumption?

How have humans affected the land itself? Is it still relatively untouched or have land formations been altered or removed entirely? Has an increase in pavement affected how well the land can absorb water, or have drought or flooding increased due to a change in absorption capacity? How easy is it to walk across the land? Have private property lines, busy roads, and other physical obstacles made it more difficult to be a pedestrian?

What is the status of native plants? Are there still areas of virgin forest or prairie? Are there invasive plant species competing with natives? Or are you in a highly cultivated area where all the plants you see were deliberately placed there by people? Does the agriculture in the area rely mostly on a few commercially popular species like corn or wheat? Is there any emphasis on heirloom and organic crops, crop rotation, permaculture, and other pre-big-agribusiness practices? How far do you have to go from home to find a tree?

How about animals? Again, what is the mix of native, domestic, and invasive animal species? Are you most likely to see small animals like insects and birds, or are you in an area where larger animals abide? Is there conflict between wildlife and expanding urban areas? What sorts of relationships do people have to domestic animals? Are they primarily property, pets, or somewhere in between?

Finally, who are the humans themselves? What cultures, races, and ethnicities are represented? What is the political climate like? How about religions? Economy? How well do minorities of any sort fare? How much contact do you have with your neighbors, and who are your primary social contacts? How densely populated is your bioregion, and what sorts of habitations do people live in? What's the ratio of residential area to commercial to farmland to undeveloped? How do people relate to non-human nature? To each other?

Keep in mind that because the types of changes people make to a place may vary even within a square mile, you may have multiple answers to each of these questions. Take your time, start close to home if you like, and work your way outward. The point is to understand how humans interact with the land and its other inhabitants, even if we go through our days blissfully unaware of these ongoing connections.

> *Emma is a biology undergraduate who recently became aware of evolutionary biology. As she has studied more about the interconnections of various living beings, not just in ecosystems but over long spans of time, she has become acutely aware of her status as a human animal. What is her place in her environment, and how have the adaptations her species developed over time been a response to her ancestors' environments? She decides to start with her home territory, and sets out on foot on her next day off to explore the things she often misses when she just drives by.*

Bioregional Totemism

So far I've spent several pages on what bioregionalism is to give you some context for this model. Now let's get into how animal totemism works in all this.

I've talked about the debate over whether or not a person can choose totems. Bioregional totemism is one of those models that is particularly flexible in this respect. The more you explore your bioregion and its inhabitants, the more you may find yourself gravitating toward certain animals and their totems as you get to know them better. The totems may even connect with you themselves as you make yourself more available. On the other hand, if no totem has connected with you yet, you may also ask a totem of your choice whose physical children are found in your bioregion to help you get to know that place better.

If you do need to make that choice, your best bet is to ask one that has a significant presence in the bioregion year-round, rather than an animal that only rarely makes an appearance, as well as an animal that you encounter on a fairly regular basis. For example, the first totem I connected with when I moved to Portland was Western Scrub Jay. The neighborhood I first moved to—and after some temporary relocation, have since returned to—is one of the oldest neighborhoods on the east side of the Willamette River. There's not much room for coyotes, cougars, and mule deer amid the old Craftsman homes and hipster hideouts, but there are many small yards and gardens that harbor a whole host of birds, and many trees planted throughout the past century.

My first week here, I remember hearing this loud "VWEEEEET! VWEEEEET! VWEEEEET!" in the trees outside the apartment. I looked out and saw a flash of blue and gray, and after a little research found that I had a scrub jay (or seven) as neighbors. I had been used to blue jays back east with a very different call and coloration.

It was as though Scrub Jay was welcoming me to my new home, albeit in a rather loud and boisterous manner. Since then, Scrub Jay and his cousin Steller's Jay have been two of the main totems that have helped me to connect with this area, Scrub Jay primarily in urban areas, and Steller's Jay farther out in the wild areas where I do a lot of hiking. Together they remind me that life abounds in this place whether I'm surrounded by humans or not, and that although some of the details of each location may be unique, every place is a good place to connect to the bioregion I am a part of now.

In both of these cases, I took notice of the physical birds first, and then I approached the totems to ask for help with making these connections. They were only too happy to oblige, being in my experience some of the more gregarious totems native to the area. And they're still my main animal totem connections here.

My relationships with Scrub Jay, Steller's Jay, and other beings here have been largely informal, in that I haven't done much in the way of complex rituals with them, though I have seen them a lot in my shamanic journeying. I feel this is in part due to the nature of the Bioregional Model of totemism. With other forms of totemism where the totems may not be native to where you live, it may take more effort to create a connection with the totem, and rituals may be one way to help that along. With bioregionalism, however, you're already immersed in a common matrix, and the relationship often comes more naturally.

If you're on the search for animal totems to help you in connecting with your bioregion, the first thing to do is to consciously be in it. Walk around outside your home. How urban or rural is the area? What physical features are there, like hills, waterways, etc.? What's the plant life like? Do you see any animals when you go out? What are the weather patterns and seasons like?

Next, you'll want to find at least one animal totem of a local species that can help you to begin connecting to the bioregion more deeply. Are there any animals you tend to notice more than others? Are some more prominent in the area? Do you feel especially interested in a particular species or population?

You may find that by simply exploring your immediate environment, a totem may present itself to help you. That's how I discovered that Scrub Jay and Steller's Jay wanted to show me around their urban and wilderness homes respectively. Their physical counterparts persistently showed up whenever I was in their home, and I kept getting a bit of a spiritual "ping" in the back of my head. Once I followed up with the totems themselves, they affirmed that they were indeed trying to get my attention—and not just because jays in general are extroverts!

If this isn't the case for you, it's fine to go in search of a totemic guide to your bioregion. Again, it's not about how big and impressive the animal is so much as its frequency and proximity. You want a totem who will be a good starting point, a "tour guide," if you will. If you keep seeing a particular species of bird or insect, for example, consider approaching their totems.

Don't worry about traveling far afield to find a totem to help you, either—bioregionalism stresses going local, and so if the totem you wish to speak to literally lives in your own backyard, don't feel you have to walk to the nearest park, let alone go out into the wilderness. Bioregional totemism is about bringing totemism home as much as you can while also acknowledging everything to which "home" is connected.

> *Mercedes has lived in little desert towns in Arizona all her life. She knows that the Sonoran desert is its own unique land, and with a little more research she finds that she is in the Gold Canyon watershed, fed by several washes and waterways with seasonal variations in water levels. She has seen many types of animals over the years, from tiny biting flies to wild javelina. However, it seems the first animal she always sees when she goes out for an early morning or moonlight hike or into her yard is the western banded gecko. She realizes that this little animal has been a sort of ambassador to this wilderness, and so she approaches*

*the totem Western Banded Gecko to help her become even
more familiar with her environment.*

You can use the guided meditation in Appendix B to
ask the totem for help with connecting to your bioregion,
and you can even meditate in a physical location where
the totem's physical counterparts are common. I also have
a ritual I like to use when I'm in such a place and want to
work with that species' totem, and I'd like to offer it as one
possible alternative.

I tend to prefer very quiet rituals when I am doing
this place-based spiritual work. It's not that I am not as
much a part of the place if I am being loud and active;
on the contrary, active hiking is one of my favorite ways
to connect to a place and its denizens and feel like I am
a part of that ecosystem, moving as one piece of a living
system. But I do find it easier to immerse myself in the
place in a ritual manner when I am still and quiet because
I make less noise myself, auditorily and kinesthetically,
and can focus more on everyone and everything else.

Help Me Come Home

Go to a safe, relatively quiet location near where the totem's children live. (Or, if you can't physically go to where
those animals live, go to a place that is accessible to you,
bringing along a symbol of them and their home. Even
your own home will work as long as you have that symbolic link.) Find a comfortable place to stand, sit, or lie

down, or walk slowly (and safely—beware of walking off cliffs, for example). Don't fret if the weather isn't perfect; do what you need to do to be warm and dry (or at least warm if you're going to make a direct connection with water, like wading or swimming), and allow any inclement weather to be a good reminder that nature isn't all about sunshine and clear skies. If the weather conditions are simply too dangerous, though, with lightning or very cold or hot temperatures, either postpone until conditions are better, or do your work indoors that day.

Some people feel the need to bring an offering when they perform rituals with totems, especially on the animals' own territory. You're certainly welcome to do this, though please be aware of the offering's potential physical impact on the place and its inhabitants. For example, I discourage the feeding of wildlife, even indirectly (leaving food instead of feeding animals by hand). It encourages them to associate humans with food, which almost always goes badly for the wildlife, and it also weakens their reliance on their own instinctual and learned hunting and/or browsing skills. If you wish to offer food, have a sort of ritual picnic in which you offer the totem the spiritual essence of the food, while eating the physical portion yourself. (There will be more discussions of offerings later in the book.)

Once you're settled, ask the place you're in to open up to you, even as you open yourself up to it; you can either do this out loud or silently. Then take some time to pay attention to what you notice with all your senses. What do you see all around you, what is the lighting like, and who else (not just human) is there with you? What do you hear, and how much or little noise is there, to include your own? Breathe deeply; do you smell anything, and what is its source? If you breathe in through your mouth, can you taste anything on the air, and is there anything safe to eat there? What do you feel if you stretch out your hands, or bare your skin to the air, and what supports you as you sit, stand, or walk? What else do you notice about this particular place you're in?

Take as much time as you need to get settled in; there's no rush. Once you're ready, focus on the totem you want to ask for help. If you've been able to see or hear your totem's physical counterparts, pay attention to what you notice. Concentrate on that totem and what you know of it and its children. What might it be like to be one of those animals in this place? What could be important to them to know about it? Do you see where they might like to live or eat? Is there anything here they might consider dangerous? Think for a bit about why these animals make their homes here.

Next, invite the totem you want help from to join you. You might say silently or quietly out loud:

[Name of totem], you and your
kin have lived here longer than I have.
I would know this land more thoroughly and deeply.
I ask you to share with me a taste of that connection,
for even though I can never
know it as well as you do,
I can know it and you more than I do now.

Allow the totem to make itself known to you as it will. You might notice the physical animals more, or you may have a vision in your mind's eye of the totem approaching. Is it the totem you specifically invited, or another? Is it more commonly found in another part of the bioregion instead of the one you're currently in?

Pay attention to what and how the totem communicates with you. You may get clear answers right away. Or the results may be more ambiguous—which simply necessitates spending more time in that place with the totem until you have a better idea of its relationship to you. It also may be that the totem decides it's not the right fit. You may end up with a completely different totem approaching you instead, or even multiple totems.

Regardless of what happens, try to keep a good record of your experiences over time. The totem may ask you to fulfill a particular task to further your goals, or it may give you important information that will come in handy in your explorations of the bioregion. Some totems are very direct; others may only give you a piece of the puzzle with each meeting. Either way, it's helpful to be able to go back and look over your work with the totem over time to note patterns and themes, as well as to see how the relationship develops along the way.

Exploring the Land, Hand in Hand—or Wing

Once you've made the initial connection with the totem, it's time to do some exploring together. Start in parts of the bioregion where the totem's children are most commonly found. If the place you have chosen seems to be a good one for connecting with the totem in question, do your best to make that a personally sacred space. Continue to use it for further communications and even ritual work if you like. However, if the totem indicates someplace else instead or in addition to your initial location, check it out as you're able to. Just try to stay within your bioregion, and the more local the better, especially early on. It's better to have a deeper understanding of a small place than a broader set of places where you only have a small connection.

Much of the direction at this point may be from the totem, who may suggest ways to connect to the land and its inhabitants. However, the following exercises may also be used as you and the totem see fit.

A Brief Report

This is a two-part exercise, and it's up to you which you want to do first.

One part involves doing as much research as possible on the behavior and other natural history of your totem's species. Books, websites, and videos are all fair game, though be aware of how reliable the source material is. You can also explore mythology and folklore about the animal, including more modern manifestations. How we view animals symbolically can have a huge impact on how we relate to them in real life; the prevalence of the Big Bad Wolf still causes many people to fear wolves unnecessarily.

The other part includes observing the animal in its habitat as much as possible, or at least studying that habitat in light of what you know about the animal. If you can observe the animal on a regular basis, compare what you see with what you read. If, on the other hand, sightings are slim to none, pay attention to what you can see of the plants, waterways, land, and other phenomena the animal is likely to interact with, and meditate on how these things contribute to what makes the animal the way it is.

In the event that you are unable to get to the part of your bioregion where your totem's physical counterparts are found, for example a remote forest, viewing videos of the animals online can substitute to a degree, especially if the footage was taken in your bioregion. Observing animals in zoos and wildlife parks is an option, too. However, be aware that a captive wild animal may behave very differently from one in the wild. Closed spaces restrict natural movement, and very few animals in captivity receive the same amount of territory they normally would have. Additionally, captivity can exaggerate certain behaviors; for example, wolves in captivity tend to exhibit more pronounced pack hierarchical activity as the pack members are in closer constant proximity

You can do either part of this exercise first. Some may prefer to watch the animal first and then plug their observations into known information. Others, especially those with less of a chance of direct observation, might choose to start with the research and then go into the field more informed. The goal either way is to be able to connect the theoretical knowledge about the animal with observation of the animal or its habitat at least.

Let's say you live in the Mojave desert, and you're working with Chuckwalla, the totem of a large desert lizard. You know that like many desert animals, the chuckwalla is mostly active at night, and the months of April and May are the height of their reproduction season before the weather gets too hot. Hiking out in the desert, you may observe the effects of the heat on you and imagine what it may be like for an animal that lives outdoors all the time. Additionally, you might take a peek at the creosote and other plants that the chuckwalla feeds on and relies on for hydration as well. If you're fortunate enough, you may get to see a chuckwalla out and about, but even if not, you've still stepped into its living room for a bit.

Through Your Eyes

This exercise takes observation to a different level. It's best done only with a totem you know you can trust: you will be invoking the totem, calling it into you for a period of time so you can experience what it is like to be that animal. It's the same concept as shapeshifting dance, a practice of ritualistically moving like the animal (discussed later), but with the added purpose of allowing you to explore your bioregion with the senses of the totem's species.

You're going to want a place you know pretty well, and where you're aware of the risks involved. This will vary, of course, as your backyard is most likely safer than a steep mountain trail. Also, be aware of the people in the vicinity. Having someone you know and trust along to let others know what's going on can help keep you from being interrupted; however, trying to do this exercise on a busy stretch of beach can not only be distracting for you, but also potentially disturbing for bystanders who are convinced you're either under distress or the influence, so choose your location wisely. Also, if your work is done in or near water, you *really, really, really* want to have someone around to keep you from accidentally falling in!

Before you try this exercise, come up with a key word or phrase that can bring you back to your human self if necessary. It might be your name and address, a few lines of poetry or prose, a bit of song. If you want to be sure to link it strongly to your humanity, spend a couple of weeks meditating on it daily, reciting the word(s) while being very conscious of your human form and awareness.

So let's say you have a relatively safe place, a human companion if necessary, and a totem you trust enough to take down your personal psychic boundaries for a little while. Get yourself comfortable, preferably sitting or lying down. Make sure your companion is aware of what you're doing and knows your key word or phrase—remind yourself of that word or phrase, too.

Clear your mind as best as you can, and focus on what you sense around you. Feel your connection to the land and its inhabitants, and remember your identity as a part of this bioregion.

When you feel ready, call on the totem to join you. Ask it to show you a bit of its experience, and what life as one of its children is like. Visualize your solar plexus opening up.

Invite the totem in. As you do, imagine that your body is shifting and changing in shape. Feel your limbs lengthen, shorten, or even multiply or disappear entirely. Feel how your weight is distributed, where your center of gravity is, and whether you are larger or smaller than you are as a human. Next, extend your awareness out through your senses. Is vision still important, or are you paying more attention to what you hear or smell?

Spend as much time as you like simply sitting or lying down while in this state. In fact, it isn't even necessary to move around at all for this to be effective. While the movement elements of shapeshifting are powerful indeed, this exercise is largely about perception. And in fact, some animals spend a lot of time staying still. Web-building spiders, for example, may sit on their webs for hours waiting patiently for food, while snakes can spend an entire afternoon basking on a warm, sunny rock.

It can take practice to get accustomed to perceiving through the totem's senses. Make sure you're used to this altered state before you try to get up and run around. If you do move, it's crucial to maintain connection to your human judgment, no matter how deeply you sink into the other animal mindset. Observe, but don't become lost.

One thing that can help is keeping your initial goal in mind. You want to be able to learn more about your bioregion from the perspective of the totem whose children live there. So allow yourself to experience that headspace, but at the same time try to "keep notes" on it from a human perspective. What seems most interesting to you as your totem animal, compared to what most catches your attention as a human? Do you notice anything new or different you missed before? What are your reactions to the place and its inhabitants like now?

It's best to keep your initial experiments short. If you're with someone, have them call you back after fifteen minutes or so, or if you seem like you're going to wander too far away. Have them do this as gently as possible, calling your name or your key word/phrase. They should avoid touching you unless necessary, as this can jar you out of that altered state too suddenly and leave you feeling disoriented.[16] It can also startle you in your totem animal mindset and cause you to panic. On the other hand, if you're getting yourself into danger, then by all means your companion should snap you back into being human.

If you're alone, have an alarm set, maybe even two different sources. If you have a smart phone, you may be able to record your key word/phrase and use it as your alarm sound. You could also keep a pocket-sized tape player or digital recorder on your person; have the recording play fifteen minutes of silence, followed by the key word/phrase repeated over and over, perhaps quietly at first and then with increasing volume.

Have some protein-rich food and water or a sports drink available for when you come back out, as this can be very intense work. Eating can help ground you again. As soon as possible after you've recovered, write down your experiences or record them. The longer you wait, the less

---

16. Have you ever felt a little distant when you've been interrupted while in deep thought? It's about like that.

you may retain. It is a good idea to keep recording your impressions over time as you're able to reflect more on what happened. They may sound a little odd to your more grounded mind, especially if you're still a bit in totem-mind when you make the recording, but those initial first records can't be duplicated.

If you feel comfortable, in subsequent practice you can try exploring more, to include moving around some. Try moving like the animal to the best of your ability, though if your totem happens to be a bird or fish, this may be a bit difficult. Just do your best, and don't worry about looking silly. It happens to all of us; we can all share in the silliness together!

One caveat: it is very important that you always maintain some connection to your humanity. In my work with totemism and related practices, I have met the occasional person who has used this sort of shapeshifting exercise as an excuse to let go of their self-control. They will act out while in the animal mind, and then blame it on that "other" mindset. They may even explain their experiences as "proof" that the totems of "vicious" animals like Wolf, or Bear, or Tiger are really "in them," and refuse any help. If you find yourself losing control in this way, your best bet is to brush up on basic meditation and other magical techniques to improve your self-control. Postpone the shifting until you can handle yourself better.

Twenty-Four-Hour Retreat

The previous two exercises most likely only took you a few hours at best, including travel time, preparation, and wrap-up. The next step is much more intensive; you will be experiencing a place in your bioregion with your totem for a twenty-four-hour period.

This will, of course, require some planning. First of all, you need to be able to set aside an unbroken twenty-four hours in which you remain in the same place as undisturbed as possible. Some places simply won't allow it; many public parks, for example, close at night, and I do not wish to advocate getting a trespassing citation! Other places may not be safe at night, especially if you're inexperienced in how to handle them. Whether the danger is from mountain lions on the hunt, or unsafe human beings, you'd best choose another place, especially if you'll be alone.

Don't let the possibility of danger hobble you too much, though. I have gone on numerous solo hikes in the mountains of Oregon, and as a rather small, unintimidating woman, I feel safe out there—I'm most likely to run into other hikers like me, not dangerous criminals. I tend to choose hikes that, although relatively remote, still have a bit of human traffic on a daily basis, which can help me reduce the risk of illness or injury without help while still allowing for some privacy on my hike. If you know someone with private property who would be willing to let you use it, it can be a good balance between safety and privacy.

The closer you can be to the actual territory of the totems' children, the better. If it's the totem of a small, fairly gregarious songbird that isn't too spooked by people, or even the earthworms in your garden, this may be relatively easy. However, with other animals it may be better to give them lots of space. Grizzly Bear is indeed a powerful totem, but camping in grizzly country can lead to disaster if you don't take the right safety precautions.

And, again, if you simply are unable for any reason to get to the place where the totem's physical children live, or are unable to stay there for an extended period of time, you can always do this exercise someplace more accessible to you. Just have a representation of the totem with you and use that as a connection to the animals' home.

Make sure you take everything you need to be comfortable, too. What will you need to eat, and how much water will you need? Where will you sleep? Will you need a way to stay warm or cool? Do you have a cell phone, and is there reception? Do you need a flashlight, a journal, toilet paper? Will trusted people know where you are in case of an emergency, and do they know when to expect you back home?

It's up to you whether or not you take someone with you. If you go alone, it's especially important that you are able to keep yourself grounded in your humanity if you decide to explore the place with the totem's senses during your retreat. Make sure your companion knows this is a spiritual retreat for you, and that you will want to stay in a relatively small area, focusing on your spiritual work.

Say you have your supplies, your companion if applicable, and you've just gotten everything set up in your chosen place. Your twenty-four hours has just begun. Now what?

Start by greeting the place and the beings that live in it. Let them know your intent and how long you'll be there, and ask for their permission to stay. This can be done as simply as asking, either silently or out loud. You can also do a more formal ritual; you can create your own, or here's one to try if you like:

- Sit or lie on the ground (if possible) when you first arrive at the place. Visualize the boundaries of your body; feel where "you" end and the rest of the world begins. Now touch the ground with your hands and feel the physical connection between your skin and the plants and earth beneath. Say silently or out loud, "Spirits of the Land of [name of place/park/ etc.], I am [name], of [place you are from]. I am here accompanied by [totem] to learn more about this place and those who live here. I ask for safe passage and a safe stay for a day and a night."

- Wait, and be open to whatever signs or feelings you may have. You may have a physical sensation such as a bit of an adrenaline rush or a cold chill. You may

see an animal appear, even briefly, or notice
other signs that may be the place giving
you recognition. Or you may simply feel relaxed,
joyous, or scared. If you feel as though you are not
welcome, you may wish to find another place that's
a better match. However, if the place feels neutral
or even welcoming, go ahead and get set up there.

• Before you stop touching the ground, if you choose
to stay there, give a bit of your energy to the place.
You can imagine a bit of yourself flowing through
your fingers into the earth. You can even leave a bit
of your physical self, such as a bit of hair. Thank the
place for letting you stay there.

Next, determine some physical boundaries beyond
which you can't go for the next twenty-four hours (except in case of emergency). What are some physical landmarks? Can you safely observe the animals themselves
nearby? If you're working with Beaver, is there a dam for
you to sit by and observe? If you can't really get a good
look at the animals where you are, if they're just too elusive or far away, then make sure you can at least get a
sense of how they might interact with the place you're in.

Generally speaking, smaller is better, because you
want more depth than breadth in your experience. It's
better to be able to get a lot of information about a relatively small space than a bunch of snippets of information

about a larger area. Even if your totem's children have a tendency toward large territories, keep your territory in close for this. Depending on the place, it may be as small as a quarter acre, though try not to make it any bigger than one square mile.

Next, spend some time wandering the place you've demarcated. At first, simply observe as a human being. Here are some starting points for observation:

- Do you see any animals here? This includes little invertebrates like insects and spiders. Do you see evidence of other creatures, such as prints, old spider webs, feathers, and the like?

- How many species of plants do you see? How many can you identify? Do you know which are native and which may be introduced or even invasive?

- Is there any water nearby? Is it naturally occurring or manmade, like an artificial pond? Is it still or running? How clean is it? Can you see any animals or plants living in it?

- What is the ground like? Is there dirt under your feet, or sand, or stone? Does it hold water for a long time, or does water evaporate quickly? Does it support a lot of plant life?

- Are there other notable natural phenomena? Do you see mountains, hills, or sand dunes? Was the land shaped by glaciers, erosion, plate tectonics, or other forces?

· How dramatic is the human influence here? Are you in a city, the wilderness, or somewhere in between? Are you alone, or are there other people around you? Are the roads big and paved, or narrower and unpaved? Do you have access to plumbing and sturdier shelter than a tent?

Once you're more familiar with the place itself, you may wish to simply relax and be in it. Some people are content with filling their retreat with meditation, breathing exercises, reading, watching the water of a stream drift by, and other relatively quiet activities. If this is your preference, that's fine. Just keep your senses open to your environment, and make sure to set aside some time to talk with the totem while you're there.

The totem may have some specific tasks for you to try out. If not, here are some suggestions:

· Use the "Through Your Eyes" exercise in the last section. Ask the totem to show you what it is about this place that appeals to its physical counterparts; or, if it doesn't live there, ask why it's not a good place. Then explore the place through the eyes of the totem, again taking all the precautions from before, especially if you're alone.

· Try your hand at nature writing. Classic nature writing is nonfiction prose that combines natural history (objective facts about the natural phenomena) with personal, subjective observations and impressions during experiences in nature. However, many people also feel moved to write poetry and even fiction when in contact with a natural place. During this retreat, try to keep it on the totem's children as much as possible, and pay attention to the environment, especially if the animals aren't present. If you're not a writer but enjoy visual arts or making music, use your preferred medium instead.

· See if there are other bioregional totems that may introduce themselves to you here. You may ask the totem who guided you here for suggestions, or you can try using the guided meditation to open yourself up to the local totems in this place.

· Check in with your surroundings every hour. How do the weather, light, and other such things change throughout the day and night? Are there times when your totem is more active or easy to contact/sense? Do these align with times when the totem's physical counterparts are most active, or times that are best in your waking/sleeping cycle?

· When you sleep, whether for a nap or for a longer period of time, be very aware of your dreams. You may even ask the totem to send you Big Dreams before you go to sleep. When you wake up, do your best to record as much of your dreams as you can. Even if you didn't have dreams, pay attention to your emotional state upon waking; even if we don't consciously remember our dreams, they can still leave their imprints on us once we're awake again.

• If you are an accomplished dreamer, actively explore where you are on the dream level. If you have shamanic experience and are able to journey, try journeying in this place and exploring it on a spiritual level. You may wish to ask permission again before exploring the place on these levels, especially the spiritual, as journeying in particular can take you into very deep and intimate parts of a place. Additionally, both the dream world and the spiritual world can be home to beings that don't really interact with the physical world at all, but which may still need to be greeted when you arrive. You can use the same greeting ritual as when you first arrived on the physical level to announce your presence and ask permission on the dream and/or spiritual levels of the place.

When it's time to leave, make sure the place is at least as clean as when you arrived; if you can leave it nicer, so much the better. Also, be aware that it may not be legal to take natural souvenirs. In the U. S., at least, there are restrictions on removing plants and animals (alive or dead) from federal and state parks without special licenses, and the removal of these beings can negatively affect the ecosystem as well as the beings themselves. Some plant and animal parts, even those that are naturally shed, may be illegal to possess due to either federal or state laws. So if you're tempted to take home a few live minnows from a creek, or a songbird or raptor feather you found, you're better off leaving it be.

> *Alex has decided to take a solo camping trip in an isolated place along the banks of the Meramec River in Missouri where he has spent a lot of time in the past hunting and fishing. Upon arriving, he greets the land, and feels it is safe to be there. Once he has set up his campsite, he walks a little way up and down the river, but feels the need to stay close to the water itself. As it is a hot summer day, he decides to go for a swim. As he does so, he sees a midland smooth softshell turtle basking on the bank. He has a feeling almost like recognition as the turtle waits for just a moment before gliding smoothly into the water.*
>
> *Over the next few hours, until the sun sets, he watches as two of these turtles feed and swim in the water, fascinated by their graceful movements. He even swims with them and pretends to be a turtle himself, though the experience seems more profound to him than the turtles going about their business despite the human splashing about in their waters. As he sleeps that night, their totem comes to*

him in a dream and introduces herself. She invites him to come back to the river whenever he can. Whether he sees one of these turtles or not, he always greets the totem, and finds safety in that place with each visit.

These three practices are just a few of the many ways in which you can gain a greater appreciation for your bioregion with the help of your totem. They're a good way to gather information and experience—but then what do you do with all of it?

For one thing, any of these exercises may be done with more than one totem over time. It's common for a person to meet more totems as their first one walks with them through their bioregion. Each totem brings its own perspective to the table, and so starting the process over with each can yield a new wealth of understanding. There are years of potential experiences just in these three exercises.

However, bioregional totemism also can be used to create a sort of avatar or archetype of bioregionalism overall, a symbol or shorthand if you will. Gray Wolf, for example, has become a well-known symbol of environmentalism, especially preservation of wild places. In the same way, a bioregional totem can act as a symbol of one's personal relationship to the bioregion. I've mentioned that we tend to associate best with beings that are most like us because relating is easier. Working with another animal can help us to connect with less familiar beings such as plant or stone totems. Animals are keenly aware of the plants, landforms, waterways, and other parts of their habitats; we often see these only as scenery as we may live in very anthropocentric habitats ourselves.

Additionally, this kind of totemism is about bringing animal totemism back around to the other animals and the habitats they live in and share with other beings. Too often totemism has been taken in a very human context, concerned with what we can get from them and how they can "empower" us. While there's value in an Archetypal Model of totemism (explored in the next chapter), all too often the animals are taken out of their niches and plugged into wherever we want them without any thought to the effect it may have on them and us. Much of modern totemism is very self-centered, which brings me to one more exercise: giving back.

Returning Balance

By now you should have a decent understanding of your bioregion if you've been doing the exercises and research. (There's always more to learn, of course.) Your research should include an understanding of the imbalances in the bioregion, particularly those brought about by humanity's enthusiasm for "progress" at the expense of everything and everyone else.

I am not a huge fan of rituals meant to rebalance the "energy" of a place that has been polluted or otherwise damaged—rituals that "wrap the *entire* world in white light," for example. I personally don't see where they're making a difference, not just because they don't actually remove the pollution or other problem in any measurable way, but also because the participants walk away once the ritual is done feeling good about themselves—and the problems still remain. Granted, it's possible to wrap a purification ritual into an ongoing effort to help a given place, but I rarely see it done.

This section, then, is really about a series of exercises and practices rather than just one. The goal is not only to understand your bioregion better, but also make real efforts on several fronts to improve it. There's no single right way to do this. The exact focus will depend on several factors, such as your specific bioregion, its needs, the resources and time available to you, the problem's severity, and so forth. Here are a few starting points to help you get going:

- How healthy is the land and the water? What about the air? What are the primary sources of pollutants and other damage? Is it primarily an industrial problem, or are individuals also contributing? Are there sources of pollution from far away outside of the bioregion, such as air pollution blown in from other places, or filthy water from upstream? Is the bioregion overdeveloped, overhunted, or just plain overpopulated?

- What efforts are underway already to try to correct these problems? How much effect have they been able to have? What stands in the way of further progress? Politics? Economy? An unsympathetic populace? An overwhelming set of problems? How can you contribute with what you have right now, either with time or money?

- What can you do on an individual, immediate basis? Are your sacred places in need of cleaning up? Can you do more around the home, such as recycling or reducing your consumption of unnecessary material goods?

- What does your totem need from you, and what does it consider important for you to focus on? Is there anything you can do to help protect its physical children and their habitat? What about the other beings it relies on, such as prey animals, plants, or symbiotic partners? What is the local human attitude toward the animals? Could they use some positive PR, or even some mention of their very existence?

I recognize that I've asked a lot of questions throughout this chapter. That's because while a lot of this book is based on personal experience, this chapter is especially so. The place you live, the beings you connect with, and where you go from there—all these are determined by you and your specific circumstances. Therefore, much of the practical material is based not on rote answers with a prefabricated setting, but in determining what you'll work with and how.

When you want to give back to your bioregion, it's best to tend to its individual needs as opposed to more broad, general work. It's like different environmental groups. Big, high-profile organizations that do a lot of government lobbying and awareness raising on a wide range of issues do a lot of good work, especially those that maximize the amount of funding raised toward actual environmental work (as opposed to higher-ups' salaries, operational costs, etc.). However, these organizations often work on national or international levels and can't always pay attention to small, localized problems.

Many areas have small, local organizations dedicated to protecting individual waterways or other habitats, or preserving and even reintroducing a particular species. They often need volunteers and funding, and if you're able to provide either or even both, you can make a significant difference to what the organization is working to protect.

Bioregional Totemism on the Move

The questions I've been asking all along are especially important to remember if you have a tendency to move frequently or spend extended vacations away from home and wish to maintain connections wherever you go. Bioregionalism began in part as a response to the increased tendency of people in the United States and elsewhere to move to new locations frequently and thereby further decrease their connection to whatever places they live.

Just as with other elements of globalization, moving isn't in and of itself a bad thing. For some people it's a necessity, or a chosen way of life. The trick is to be aware of places as you move through them, and to be able to make connections regardless of the circumstances.

Bioregionalism is a really good tool for this. The aforementioned artificial boundaries such as state lines simply don't have the same visceral, emotional impact of shifts from one bioregion to the next. A sign saying "Welcome to Oregon!" doesn't have quite the same appeal to me as the drive down Highway 26 from Portland to Bend, where in a space of just a few miles I watch the Cascades melt away into desert.

There's no such thing as too little time to get to know a place, if you have enough time to set foot in it (outside of, say, a climate-controlled airport, bus station, or hotel). One of my fondest memories is going to PantheaCon, a Pagan convention in San Jose, and having a dear friend of mine introduce me to the Guadalupe River, which flows near the convention's hotel. I had been to the convention in years previous, but had never had any reason to leave the hotel once I arrived because my room and all the activities were there. We went for a walk, though, and while the river was small, and surrounded by Big City, I could feel the heartbeat of the place pulsing through it. We only spent perhaps half an hour there, but it changed my connection to the place.

If you're in a place only for a period of weeks or months, you probably won't get nearly the connection that you would if you lived there for years. Additionally, it should also be mentioned that just because you have the skills to connect to a place, it doesn't mean the connection will happen. Sometimes there are just fundamental barriers and dislikes that prevent it. For example, I am a not a fan of huge metropolises. Portland is about as big a city as I want to live in. I tried Seattle for a year, and it was just too much. I can't even imagine living in Los Angeles, where my partner hails from, even though he assures me there are plenty of pockets of open space, including the coastline. It was also telling that Portland and the surrounding region had two totems who connected to me almost immediately, while Seattle had none the entire year I was there.

I do try my best to connect to places when I visit them or live there temporarily. And bioregional totemism can be a useful foot in the door, as it were. In fact, if you can introduce yourself successfully to a totem of that area before you arrive, it can further the land's acceptance of you.

There are a few ways of making that initial introduction. Many animals are native to multiple bioregions, even in places that are far away from each other. In every place I've lived there have been robins, and so Robin has been a constant presence whether I lived in the East, the Midwest, or the Pacific Northwest; the same can be said of Raccoon, Whitetail Deer, Honeybee, Wolf Spider, and many others. On occasion, I've asked these common totems to help me integrate into a new place.

Another option is to ask people who have long connected to the land you're going to for suggestions on totems to work with. They may have suggestions of which ones may be more amenable to you essentially dropping in on them, and which are better left alone, at least at first.

You can also do a little preliminary exploration. Regardless of how you find an introductory totem, it's a good idea to go in with some basic research about the new bioregion already under your belt. This information can be helpful in identifying an animal whose totem you can ask for help.

If you want to try before you travel, you can use a guided meditation to go spiritually to the new place and seek out the totem there, whether it's a totem someone else suggested or one you've chosen to approach yourself. Remember that you are a guest there for the time being and have not yet reached "resident" status. Here's a brief sample you may use:

- Go to a place where you feel truly at home and connected, to the best of your ability. Make yourself comfortable, clear your mind, and relax.

- Visualize yourself flying, running, or even swimming to the border of the bioregion you will be going to. Stop at the border. If you have chosen to bring a spiritual offering, uncover it and place it there now.

- Call to the totem that you wish to help you. You might try saying the following:

[Name of totem], I stand at the edge of your home here, this [forest/desert/etc.] where you dwell.
In [such and such period of time], I intend to come to this place whole, in body and spirit alike.
As a traveler and newcomer, I ask for safe entry and a safe place to stay.
In the time that I am fortunate enough to be here, I wish to be a part of this land as much as I can.
I ask for your help in being of this place, you who have been here so much longer than I.
Let this be a mutually beneficial meeting; let me enhance the land even as it nurtures and supports me.
Will you be my help in this endeavor?

As always, pay close attention to the totem's response. The totem may agree to help you and invite you in, or it may direct you to a different totem to help you. Use the time between now and your relocation to work with the totem to prepare for your arrival. The totem may want you to find out more about the land and its inhabitants and perhaps even prepare offerings to bring with you. You may also ask the totem to help with logistical issues, for example, finding a job or home in the new place to make the actual move smoother.

There is the possibility, albeit relatively small, that it may refuse to help you at all and even act as though to prevent your entry. If the latter is the case, don't take it as a reason to cancel your plans (especially if doing so would create significant difficulties in your physical life, such as if your employer is sending you to this place). However, you may need to make your good intentions clearer or find out why the totem is being hostile. In the event that you end up going to the place anyway, you may find that it initially doesn't welcome you, and you may even run into difficulties. If this happens, don't be discouraged. Instead, try to find out if there is a particular reason for the initial incompatibility. The place may simply need more time to get to know you, or there may have been a piece of etiquette you haven't observed. Finding out what you need to do may require asking around; try approaching local Pagans and other spiritual folk, in addition to totems you haven't contacted yet.

Hopefully you'll make the connection sooner or later and can proceed with some of the exercises described earlier. You'd be surprised how much you can learn about a place you're connected to, even if it's just for a short time. The most important thing is to be observant and curious.

Seek out any source of information and experience about the bioregion. In doing so, you may greatly enrich your time in this place, whether it's a permanent move or a temporary visit.

Beyond the Animal Totem

By now, I hope you understand that animal totems don't inhabit a vacuum—they are the spiritual manifestations of animals that live as interwoven parts of complex ecosystems. While I highlight animal totems because of their closeness and familiarity to us, they are a bridge to knowing other parts of a bioregion physically and spiritually.

You are certainly welcome to continue focusing on animal totems; plenty of people do with great success. However, there are also the totems of plants and stones and such, and the *genii locorum* (spirits of entire places), to be met and worked with. Animal totems are a good reminder to us that we, too, are animals. They also remind us that we can reclaim our place in the natural order, attempting to restore what we have destroyed while retaining the best of our unique creations as a species.

Most importantly, I hope both the bioregionalism and the totemism discussed in this chapter help you to connect. That's what this is all about. So many of us live in an increasingly isolated society, and this isolation is dangerous. Reaching out to another being—whether human, animal, or a different spirit entirely—is one way to counteract unhealthy trends of detachment. Take this material where you will, but remember that you are never alone in it.

Elliot has spent a couple of years working with Bullfrog to learn more about the wetlands near his home. He originally started working with the totem because he had been fascinated by the loud, booming croaks of the bullfrogs he heard at night. Over time, Bullfrog introduced him to many of the plants and other animals in the ecosystem, and encouraged Elliot to learn more about how they all worked together. Even the sand and the mud were important, as he found out. Today, Elliot is the head of a newly formed wetlands conservation group working to improve the water quality there and enhance the health of the ecosystem as a whole, as well as educate people about the ecological benefits of wetlands to the greater area. The bullfrogs are some of the most sensitive residents of these wetlands, and they have seen healthier numbers in population as a direct result of less pollution and cleaner water. Bullfrog is pleased.

Further Resources

What I have offered in this chapter is just one small set of ideas and practices for a more ecologically centered spirituality. There are many other books and resources available if you want to expand the tools available to you. However, if I had to pick just three books, here's what I'd suggest:

Coming Back to Life: Practices to Reconnect Our Lives, Our World by Joanna Macy and Molly Young Brown—I first encountered this world when I was studying ecopsychology while working on my master's degree. While it is not precisely a Pagan book, it is full to the brim of rituals meant to foster connection not only with other people, but with the rest of the world. The Council of All Beings is an especially powerful and poignant group ritual, and there are numerous options for groups, though some concepts may be adapted to individual work.

The Earth Path: Grounding Your Spirit in the Rhythms of Nature by Starhawk—I feel this book is one of Starhawk's less appreciated works. It is a phenomenal blend of commentar and meditation on the cycles of seasons and element, and it supports a particularly sustainable way of life that takes into account the numerous ways we affect the environment around us every day. Refreshingly, it lacks the guilt and shame often found in texts urging us to change our ways. Instead, it is incredibly inviting and supportive, making it even easier to approach environmental and other problems with a solution-focused mindset.

Ecoshamanism: Sacred Practices of Unity, Power & Earth Healing by James Endredy—This is one of my very favorite books. I had the great fortune to work with the author a few years ago during that trip to Sedona, and I have to say he is one of the most grounded and genuine people I've met. His approach brings shamanism back from New Age crystal-waving and "cultural neutrality" and returns it to its roots in the land. While his experiences stem from indigenous training, the text is invaluable to a postindustrial, nonindigenous culture in desperate need of reconnecting. Whether you're specifically interested in shamanism or not, this book is a must-have.

Five

The Archetypal Model of Totemism

Note: Although this chapter deals with psychological concepts and the author has a master's degree in counseling psychology, neither this chapter nor the rest of the book should be seen as psychological or medical advice, and none of this material is a replacement for past, present, or future treatment from your own health care professionals.

If the bioregional model of totemism is most concerned with outreach and connection with the world around you, the Archetypal Model is its balance, primarily concerned with the internal landscape of the psyche. My original name for it was the psychological model, but I felt that was a bit too limiting. While the individual's psychological makeup is an important part of this model, so is the shared human experience.

We are not islands, at least not in the sense of being isolated. People forget that water is a matrix that connects; the wave that washes up on one shore includes molecules that were thousands of miles away a short time ago. While an island may be a distinct land mass, it is connected to all other land masses by the water, as well as the sea floor. In the same way, while we are bounded by our skins and brains, we are all connected externally by the environment we share, and internally by human nature.

While each of us gets to write our own story as life unfolds, we're all starting with the basic template of being in human bodies, with human brains. That's a commonality we all share. Our manner of perception—being primarily visual creatures, bipedal, and mostly oriented along a vertical axis—is another important component of this shared experience. For example, the common shamanic motif of the World Tree/Mountain/other vertical axis reflects the importance we place on the way we perceive the world. If we were lower to the ground and depended more on our senses of smell, a human shaman might instead follow a flat radiating star of scents. In the same way, the archetypes we work with and the collective unconscious—

our shared human consciousness—reflect elements of the unique human experience.

When Carl Jung spoke about the roots of archetypes, he was identifying instincts and responses hardwired into humanity in general. Unlike some later interpretations of Jung's collective unconscious, there's nothing mystical or mysterious or even extrasensory about this beyond the normal range of human sense and sensation. I *don't* feel it's inferior to the practice of acknowledging some higher power or the idea that archetypes exist independently of us. But understanding the contributions of human nature to our spiritual concepts gives them their bones, the framework they're built upon. Again, we are animals, and I believe it's constructive to ground our spirituality in our animal selves.

The Archetypal Model of totemism is meant to access several layers of consciousness ranging from the shared human experience we inherit through our species and the unique structure of our brains and neurochemistry to our experiences and perceptions as individuals, and our self-understanding. It matches our internal impulses and instincts to what we know of nonhuman animals, creating a personalized map of both the internal self and the world we inhabit.

Before we go further, I want to make a note about literal versus metaphorical interpretations of archetypal totemism. Throughout this book I use language that alternately refers to totems either as individual autonomous beings or as internal symbols. This chapter is especially concerned with totems as symbols, and in its purest form archetypal totemism is about the creation and development of metaphors—not actual beings—so much of the language and concepts will reflect this. If you also believe totems are literal beings in addition to being symbolic, please do not feel that this chapter is only useful from a metaphorical perspective; instead, see it as one of many ways of understanding and working with the totems.

What Are Archetypes?

When called upon to explain what totems are in a nutshell, my preferred answer is "archetypal beings that embody all the qualities of a given species." My experience with them has shown them to be overarching manifestations akin to deities, rather than individual spirits. That's why I refer to "Gray Wolf" or "Whitetail Deer" as opposed to "a wolf totem" or "a deer totem." I'm not working with a spirit that may have once lived in a physical body, but something that is more akin to a deity, a force in and of itself in animal form. Gray Wolf, for example, is not just "made of" all the natural history and behavior of physical gray wolves, but also relationships wolves have with other species, to include humans. We add to the makeup of Wolf as totem as well with our lore and legends about wolves.

What are often referred to as archetypes in Neopagan and related spiritualities are in some ways far departed from the original psychological concept of archetypes espoused by Carl Jung. This pioneering psychoanalyst did invaluable work with defining and utilizing archetypes in therapeutic practice. His emphasis was on archetypes as manifestations of elements of the human consciousness. Archetypes are the map showing the territory of human impulses, drives, and needs; they stem from the part of the brain that speaks in symbols. Jung used these archetypes as models of different parts of the human psyche to help patients have a better understanding of themselves as individuals as well as being part of the human species. Archetypes inhabit the collective unconscious, the part of our unconscious mind that reflects both shared biology and neurochemistry, as well as inherited behaviors and psychological makeup from our human and previous ancestors.[17]

In this way, Jung created a map for exploring the territory of how our minds work. While we are all individuals, as human beings we have inherited certain biological, neurochemical, and behavioral patterns that were developed through thousands upon thousands of generations of human and older ancestors. From the physical structure of our brains, to our tendency to be social creatures, to the

---

17. Carl Jung, *Man and His Symbols* (Garden City, NY: Doubleday and Company, 1964).

reactions of our adrenaline system when we are startled—these are all our animal heritage. Jung mapped out some of these impulses through archetypes, complex symbols of how the impulses could manifest in the human life.

So for example, the Shadow, one of Jung's better-known archetypes, embodies some of the earlier, more primitive instincts and impulses we have as animals, particularly aggressive or defensive ones. It may manifest as our weakest parts, the things that are least admirable in us, or that are the least socially acceptable, and the Shadow is prone to projecting our weaknesses onto others. A person who feels insecure about their ability to bring in enough money at their job may lash out at coworkers and try to be overly competitive with them. This reflects the tendency of animals to compete with each other for scarce resources, and fails to make use of the more socially advanced ways in which some humans (and other animals) have found to resolve conflicts both between each other and within the self.

This is part of why it is so important to keep the internal source of archetypes in mind when working with them. The popular conception of archetypes commonly found in Neopaganism, New Age practices, and so forth, too often focuses so much on the externalized map that the original internal territory is lost from view. It is true that archetypes often take on a life of their own, given power by our belief in them. But that belief is fueled by our recognition of ourselves within them, and the "relationship" on its most fundamental level. We lose sight of the basic elements of human nature that archetypes *represent*, glorifying the messengers rather than the powers that sent them out into the waking world. The Shadow is not some vague being outside of ourselves, but a deeply ingrained part of who we are. If we treat it as an external being, then we have given up the most important tool in dealing with it—self-knowledge.

It is important to remember that no matter how real they are to us, the archetypes themselves are still maps—representations of our deeper, internal impulses and the drives of the human psyche. Exploring and working with archetypes can be an incredibly rich and beautiful experience, but if we lose sight of their origins and which parts of ourselves they describe, we run the risk of getting lost in fantasy worlds detached from ourselves and the world we live in.

> *Martin is trying to work with Wolverine; he was initially attracted to Wolverine's individualistic image and the idea of Wolverine as a lone warrior. Since he wants to be more like this totem, he begins to isolate himself, especially when it comes to his work. He pushes himself harder and harder not to rely on anyone else, until one day he finds himself entirely burned out, with no one to help him.*
>
> *Upon reflection, he realizes that he had idealized Wolverine's individuality, and in doing so damaged his much-*

needed social network. Was this really what he needed? What was really causing him to feel so competitive, and to feel such a strong need to succeed by his own power?

Martin was focusing primarily on the image of Wolverine as the lone warrior, without looking at what that represents in the human psyche. What impulse or desire is behind that archetype? Perhaps it is the social mammalian tendency to leave the family group at a certain age and start one's own community, and the need to prove oneself as a distinct being. Looking at the internal source of the archetype and the feelings you associate with it can give you more insight into and awareness of yourself and your actions, and help you to make better decisions with regards to the part of yourself that resonates with the archetype. It also allows you to take yourself in context, to include not just who you are, but your environment, human and otherwise.

The Archetypal Model of totemism is an attempt to reconnect that very externalized conception of animal totems with the parts of the psyche they resonate with by starting with the psyche itself. In the example with Wolverine, Martin was trying to fit certain traits into his life because he thought he was being like Wolverine. He was trying to fit himself into the archetype, instead of seeing how the archetype fit into his own psyche. He was so focused on an idealized external Wolverine as the Warrior archetype that he neglected to see whether that was a good fit for his own psyche.

A Few Mapmakers

The field of psychology is full of people who have parceled the human psyche into portions as a way of more detailed study and understanding. Some of these, such as Carl Jung, have drawn on other disciplines, such as religion and mythology, to create their maps of the mind. While this chapter should not be seen as the be-all and end-all discussion of these concepts, I'd like to introduce them as examples and potential inspiration.

Carl Jung

Carl Jung's archetypal theory is among the best-known psychological models used in Neopagan and related spiritualities. As discussed above, he considered archetypes to be symbolic "beings" that were projections of basic human impulses and desires worked into symbolic forms our consciousness could more easily grasp. While many people, particularly many Neopagans, New Agers, and the like have a tendency to externalize archetypes, classically they are wholly from within the human psyche.

In his early career, Jung spent several years under the mentorship of Sigmund Freud, the founder of psychoanalysis. The two men spent a great deal of time trading notes with one another, though Freud was older and had a much more thoroughly developed approach.

Freud had his own structural model of mapping the psyche consisting of the ego, the superego, and the id. The ego is the "face" we all put on to the world around us, the mediator between not only the superego and the id, but also between the self and the environment. The superego is the controlling element of the psyche that uses shame and attention to social boundaries to keep the rest in line; it is sometimes said to be our conscience. The id is the opposite; it is pure impulse and desire, instinct and need. The id is the earliest part of the psyche to develop; a baby is all need and want, and it is only later in life that other, more mediated parts of the psyche develop.

Jung and Freud parted ways before the latter had fully developed the structural model of the psyche. However, Jung had an earlier topographical model created before the split; this model included the well-known conscious, preconscious, and unconscious minds. (By the way, these do not directly correspond to the superego, ego, and id, though the structural model was developed to address and clarify confusions people had with the earlier, topographical model.) No doubt there was discussion between Freud and Jung about how to divide up the psyche into distinct, interacting parts.

Jung strayed far away from classic psychoanalysis. He focused particularly on dream analysis to a degree that

Freud and his ilk had not. Whereas Freud's central theory of dream interpretation was that dreams were the manifestations of unfulfilled desires, Jung had a much more complex and diversified conception of the role that dreams play in the human psyche. For Jung, dreams were the landscape for a variety of not only desires, unfulfilled and otherwise, but also for a lifelong communication with the self in all its parts with its own languages and laws.

Archetypes are only one part of Jung's methods of dream analysis, but they are what we're most concerned with here. You may have heard of the Animus and Anima, the Mother Goddess, and, of course, the Shadow. These are just a few of the primary archetypes Jung identified as showing up repeatedly in human dreams and, by extension, our myths and motifs. Here's a brief overview of some of the more common archetypes; you may find these useful when exploring your own psyche.

The primary archetypes Jung described were:

- The Self: This is the whole self, the union of all levels of a person's consciousness. Jung described the process of individuation as the journey a person takes in unifying the parts of the self more fully.

- The Shadow: This contains a person's hidden, sometimes chaotic drives; like Freud's id, the shadow is wild and doesn't care for social niceties, only gratification. Working with one's shadow can be some of the most challenging internal work.

- The Animus and Anima: While constrained by a binary idea of sex and gender that only acknowledges male/masculine and female/feminine, these archetypes are twins in balance. Jung's original idea was that the animus in women and the anima in men were the "true selves" that were most connected to the collective unconscious, and that the perfect balance of animus and anima, the syzygy, was a unification that resolved conflicts.

- The Persona: Like Freud's ego, the persona is the mask we show to the world. It is not the true self but a carefully mediated presentation that shifts subtly depending on setting and company.

There are several others; these are some of the more common ones. You may recognize them in world mythology, folklore, fairy tales, and even modern fiction.[18]

---

18. Mythologist Joseph Campbell was heavily influenced by Jung's work. If you're interested in further exploration of archetypes as manifest in storytelling from prehistory onward, Campbell's works, particularly the *Masks of God* series, *The Hero With a Thousand Faces*, and *The Power of Myth*, are a good start. Do be aware that Campbell has plenty of flaws, most notably turning a very blind eye to the individual nuances and flavors of each culture's while trying to promote the idea of a universal "monomyth." Still, for the purposes of exploring archetypes in myth, Campbell is a respectable resource.

- The Triple Goddess: Jung tended to collect deities into groups of three; the Triple Goddess, consisting of the Maiden, Mother, and Crone triad is a well-known archetypal variant. Many triads of specific deities such as Persephone, Demeter, and Hecate from Greek mythos have been placed (or occasionally shoehorned) into this template by Jung and others. The Maiden, Mother, and Crone all represent not just stereotyped developmental stages in a woman's life, but also certain concepts in their own right. For example, the Maiden is innocence and potential, the Mother is fecundity and nurturing, and the Crone is wisdom and experience. The Crone is analogous to Jung's Wise Old Man, who is also a dispenser of knowledge and temperance, as well as sometimes the keeper of a crucial component in getting a strong need met.

- The Trickster: Sometimes known as the Devil, this archetype is the element of chaos, unpredictability, and the helplessness of the human condition. The Trickster also often is a reminder of humility, vulnerability, and even danger.

- The Hero: Saving the day!—or village, imperiled victim, or whatever needs saving. This is the archetype that protects and guards, being brave when no one else can.

- The Child: Like the Maiden, the Child is innocence and potential, playfulness, and a person's early, formative parts.

- The Wise Old (Wo)Man: As mentioned above, this archetype is the keeper of wisdom and guidance, and often provides assistance at crucial moments in a person's journey. For Jung, this archetype represented the completed Self at the pinnacle of individuation. Referred to in classic Jungian terminology as the *Senex*.[19]

Jung mentioned several other archetypes, and others following in his footsteps have identified still more. Jung's *The Archetypes and the Collective Unconscious* is a good starting point, and many of his works are helpful in this regard. Study the archetypes, especially Jung's main four or five, and see if you can identify yourself in any or even all of them. This is a good start to being able to understand the parts of yourself better.

With regards to working with totems, the various archetypes you identify with may be embodied in the symbolism of animals. For example, you may feel that your

---

19. Jung, *Man and His Symbols*; Carl Jung, *The Archetypes and the Collective Unconscious* (Princeton, NJ: Princeton University Press, 1981); Steven A. Mitchell and Margaret J. Black, *Freud and Beyond: A History of Modern Psychoanalytic Thought* (New York: Basic Books, 1995.)

Self is Albatross, long-soaring and long-lived, able to use wisdom and endurance that come with age to balance out all your parts. Your Shadow might be Tarantula Hawk, a wasp that paralyzes tarantulas and lays an egg in the still-living spider; the larva hatches out and eats the spider alive—and what happens when your own uncontrolled impulses and other shadowy bits manage to get the best of *you*? Your Animus or Anima could be Whitetail Deer, the true self hidden back behind the forests everyone can see easily. And your Persona could be Mimic Octopus, who not only changes color but also shape and even behavior in order to best blend in with a given environment. You could continue in this manner with other archetypes corresponding to different totems.

Developmental Psychology

Humans have long celebrated rites of passage that mark a person's shift from one stage of life to the next, though often this was done to mark more obvious changes such as puberty or childbirth. While these are very physical changes, many of them correspond with shifts in human psychology as well. Developmental psychology is the study of how our mental and emotional makeup and our brains change over the span of a lifetime. It is an incredibly useful tool to augment our understanding of what's going on in our heads from birth to death. While the stages of development are not always strictly aligned with psychological archetypes, understanding how the human being develops over time can give more insight as to where some of the archetypes came from, especially those linked strongly to specific life stages. Additionally, some later models of developmental psychology actively incorporate archetypes into their life stages.

A lot of the study of development, particularly when dealing with children, has to do with unfolding psychological abilities and knowing what a person's limitations are at a given age. It has been understood for millennia in various cultures worldwide that a person is not considered capable of certain tasks until they have passed the appropriate rite given to people when they reach a particular age; if two twelve-year-olds go through the same adulthood ceremony and one passes and the other does not, the former will be given the responsibilities of an adult while the latter will continue to be treated as a child.

There are a lot of things we simply aren't capable of until a certain point in our development. A toddler who stands in front of a television and blocks everyone else's view isn't deliberately being an obstacle; children that young simply aren't able to comprehend the idea that not everyone can see exactly what they're looking at (in this case, the television screen). And we don't begin to develop the ability to think about abstract concepts until around age eleven. So the tasks of the aforementioned rite of passage often test whether a twelve-year-old has reached a certain mental capacity required to be an adult in that society. It may not be a matter of one person being better than another; it is more a matter of one developing faster psychologically than others.[20]

There are dozens of theories of development; one of the best known is that of Erik H. Erikson. Erikson divided a person's life into eight stages, each with its corresponding conflicts and challenges. All but the last two stages are concentrated in the first eighteen years of life, leaving adults apparently mostly interested in work and having children or otherwise nurturing and providing for others, while elder adults face the challenge of dealing with fading physical and mental abilities, and facing potential regrets at having most of their lives gone.[21]

While Erikson's model does not leave a lot for anyone beyond adolescence compared to his many stages for children, the basic concept of life stages is a very useful one.

---

20. There are, of course, countless other factors at play, ranging from physical health and ability, to family support and social status. Physical limitations and a person's environment, especially as a child, can have a huge effect on how "normally" that person develops psychologically.

21. William Crain, *Theories of Development: Concepts and Applications*, 5th ed. (Upper Saddle River, NJ: Pearson/Prentice Hall, 2005). If you want to find out more about Erikson's stages, there's a ton of information for free online; a simple Google search will bring up plenty of information. And if you like books, almost any library, at least in the U.S., should have books on basic psychology that include some information on developmental psychology, if not even more resources than that.

My personal favorite model of developmental psychology isn't so well known as Erikson's, but I believe it's much more appropriate to this sort of spiritual work. In his book *Nature and the Human Soul*, Bill Plotkin creates an eight-stage model of human psychological development of his own called the Wheel of Life. Rather than basing on set age groups and neurobiological development, his stages lead a person through the process of individuation while also cultivating inner awareness and an appreciation for one's place in a larger interconnected system of life (which may appeal to those of you especially fond of the bioregional model) Like Erikson's stages, the Wheel of Life also lays out the tasks and challenges often associated with each stage. Unlike Erikson, Plotkin does not strictly associate each stage with a set age group, but instead allows that every person will pass through each stage at his or her own pace; additionally, while a person may be primarily located in one stage, he or she may still be working on some tasks from a previous stage, so the boundaries between stages are more permeable and organic. Finally, he loosely connects each stage to the age groups more evenly arched across the lifespan instead of being concentrated primarily in childhood.[22]

It would be impossible for me to do justice to Plotkin's beautiful creation in a brief summary here; instead I

---

22. Plotkin, 2008.

strongly recommend picking up a copy or recommending your library acquire it if they do not have it already. No matter what model of human development you use, the possibility for a lifetime of totemic work is quite strong.

Start by looking at where you are in your life now and reflecting on where you've been. Can you think of any rites of passage you've been through that you feel mark your moving from one stage of your life to the next? Do any existing models of developmental psychology described here or elsewhere seem to fit your experience, or do you need to make your own stages?

Keep in mind that stages of development neither have to be tied to physical development nor to mundane accomplishments. Some people only think in terms of specific ages (especially those associated with legal privileges like driving or drinking alcohol), or common experiences like graduations, major relationship changes, new jobs, moving residence, and so forth. What's important is that you feel you shifted over to a new stage of living at a particular point in your life. You may not find any real meaning in having turned eighteen or having been at a job for a year, but you may realize that the day your parents showed you how to change your car's oil was the day you felt you had earned enough independence to be an adult. Or you might have had an amazing experience during a hike or camping trip where you felt truly connected to nature and from that day on you saw yourself as an integral part of the world. My own life changes involves seven year cycles; I have noticed significant changes in my life at the ages of seven, fourteen, twenty-one, twenty-eight—and I anticipate thirty-five should be a big one as well.

You might try mapping out your life thus far, perhaps creating a timeline from birth to the present day. Think about the most significant experiences you've had, the ones where you felt you were never the same afterwards. Mark them down on the timeline, even if the spaces between them may vary quite a bit (for example, Experience A happened three years before Experience B, but Experience C happened just two months after B).

Diana is creating a timeline of her life to mark the most important and life-changing experiences she's had. Some of these are sad; her grandfather's death when she was seven was the point when even as a child she learned to accept that sometimes things don't go the way you want, but you keep on living your life anyway. The breakup with her fiancé a year ago was also a very difficult transition, though it also gave her the opportunity to live alone for the first time in her life; she discovered that she is more independent than she had given herself credit for. There are lots of good things, too. A very important rite of passage was the first time she went kayaking by herself and spent an entire day exploring a huge lake out in the wilderness. This opened her up to the beauties of nature as more than just scenery; it was a living system that surrounded and encompassed her. And while her high school graduation had been nothing special, graduating with her bachelor's degree a few years later felt like a greater accomplishment because she had been able to choose the subjects of her study herself.

Next, see if any animals seemed to really stand out in a particular stage, especially if you had definite contact with totems at that point. For example, Gray Wolf came to me when I was about two years old and was my only totem until my teen years, when Mustang came in and helped me get through the awkward period of time from about eleven to eighteen. Wolf came back after that point, and although she has always been there to some extent, in this latest period of my life as a no-longer-twenty-something adult, Brown Bear, who has also been a frequent presence, has really stepped forward to help me mature even further. There has been a lot of overlap among these and others in each stage, though; there's no set number of totems one must have at any point in life.

I tend to recommend not trying to divine what totems may show up in the future. Not only does it set up expectations, but the future is an unwritten page. As with any divination, any factor can shift and change the outcome; nothing is set in stone. Instead, if you're going to look to developmental psychology as a potential model for archetypal totemism, either look for totems that act as general symbols for developmental stages or focus on the totems you've already worked with. Learn from the lessons the totems of past stages have taught you, and implement that wisdom and knowledge in the present; the future will unfold itself all in good time.

Spiritual Mapmaking from the Inside Out

While working with preexisting sets of archetypes and categorizations can be helpful, you may wish to simply dive right into your psyche, see what it presents to you, and then use that raw material to create your own map of archetypes and symbols. You may wish to do this entirely independently, or you could also use other systems for inspiration. Either way, the rest of this chapter is dedicated to helping you sketch and then flesh out a map of your psyche using totems as representations of different parts of yourself.

The process of mapping out your psyche in totemic symbolism has a few steps to it:

- Know thyself: have a basic understanding of yourself, in part and in whole.

- Gather information: learn about a variety of animals and how others have perceived them as symbols.

- Put it together: match the totems to different elements of yourself.

· Follow the map: work with the totems as metaphors for working with your different aspects, and adjust as needed.

These do not have to be strictly linear. In the process of fine-tuning your map, you may find yourself going back to the earlier steps of finding out more about yourself and the totems in order to create a more accurate match. In fact, it's quite possible to spend your entire life reworking and changing your map as you change as a person and as your understanding of totems and the rest of the world develops over your lifetime.

Again, there's no set amount of time each step is supposed to take. You may find that you already have a good idea of your psyche's territory, for example, but need a significant amount of time to find just the right totems with which to map it out. So don't worry about deadlines or time limits—they don't apply here.

Let's go over each step in more detail now.

Know Thyself

Because so much of archetypal totemism is about mapping the psyche, your internal landscape is a good starting point. After all, you need to observe what you're making a map of before you can figure out how to best represent it.

History is full of philosophies, spiritualities, and other systems meant to increase self-awareness. One of the simplest is to ask yourself a lot of "why" questions. Why do you feel a certain way about a particular thing? Why do you respond to certain experiences the way you do? Why do you like this approach, and not that one?

It's especially important to consider things where you feel conflicted, of two (or more!) minds. We're often told that in order to be genuinely committed to an idea or decision, we have to be 100 percent sure about it. However, the reality is that we go through life with a lot of ambiguity, which is actually pretty normal. Mapping your psyche can be helpful in resolving these apparent conflicts. You won't be choosing one viewpoint over another; instead you will see that you have valid reasons for both/all of them.

The following exercises are meant to help you get a better understanding of who you are and what motivates you.

The Self-Interview

This starts out relatively simple: ask yourself a single "why" question about yourself, such as "Why does it make me sad to see others hurting?" or "Why do I like creating art?" Don't overthink the answer; just allow the thoughts to come as they will—a stream of consciousness, if you're familiar with the concept. Once you have an answer, follow it up with another "why" question, either to clarify the answer or find out more about it. Keep following answers with questions until you feel you've exhausted the trail, and then start all over again with a fresh "why" question.

Here's one sample of how this self-interview can go:

Why does it make me sad to see others hurting?
Because I don't like seeing others hurt.
Why don't I like seeing others hurt?
Because I know what it's like to be hurt,
and I don't want other people to go through that.
Why don't I want other people
to go through that?
Because I'd rather see them feeling good.
Why do I want to see them feeling good?
Because when others are feeling good, it means
that in that moment everything's okay.

The next set of questions/answers might be:

Why do I like creating art?
Because it's fun.
Why is it important to have fun?
Because I need time to relax.
Why do I need time to relax?
Because if I don't relax, I'll burn out.
Why don't I want to burn out?
Because burning out means that I enjoy life
less and am not able to accomplish as much.

And so forth. Some of the answers you come up with may seem pretty obvious and self-evident. However, the more you probe into your psyche, the more surprising things you may discover. Again, take your time. You don't have to spend hours at a time doing this. You might even try doing one interview session a day for just a few minutes, starting with a new question each time or picking up from the last one, especially if you felt stuck trying to answer it the day before.

The Self-Conversation

Here's where you get to explore those ambiguities I mentioned earlier. This exercise builds on the previous one, only this time you are identifying two distinct voices in your psyche—they're still you, but you're going to separate them based on their disagreement on a topic.

Identify something where you feel you're of a mixed mind, or where you feel you react in two or more ways at the same time. Think of each mindset individually and what makes it distinct. Then give each one a very simple designation in your mind, such as a letter or color, but don't get any more detailed than that. You just want something to help you keep these differing parts of yourself temporarily distinct.

Now, have a conversation among them. Here's one way that could happen.

> A: *I really want to go for this new job opening that just came up. I could really use the money.*
> B: *Yeah, but I also feel very comfortable in my current job. I know the people and I like the work; it just doesn't pay very well.*

A: *Well, what do I do? I'm barely scraping by right now. If there's some emergency, I have no savings to fall back on.*
B: *Is it worth the longer commute, and going into a job I might hate?*

A: *The money would make it worth it.*
B: *Am I so sure about that? Will that make it easier to get through eight or more hours a day doing something I loathe?*

You don't necessarily have to come to a resolution. Just being honest about the fact that you don't have one single way to approach a situation or concept is enough for now. The point is to be more comfortable with ambiguity and know that it isn't a bad thing. Again, it may also be a really good learning experience in the process of getting to know yourself better.

My Masks

When people think of masks, they generally think of a false face. I think of it more as a representation of a particular angle of the self. We are complex beings who take on multiple roles in everyday life, and most of us respond differently to each person in our lives. Many of us would not have the same boundaries with our parents that we do with coworkers. Even if we feel we are basically the same person in every situation, we still have to amend our boundaries as needed.

So in this case, a mask is not a false front we put up, but a symbol of the set of boundaries, mannerisms, and language we use in a particular situation or with a specific person or people. Yes, it's a matter of artificially dividing yourself up (but this is only temporary), understanding each of the parts, and then putting them back together to have a greater understanding of the whole.

Think about all the various masks you wear and roles you may adopt: parent, child, sibling, significant other, friend, coworker, teacher, student, and so forth. Then think of how those specifically manifest in your life; you may have two parents, but wear a slightly different mask for each depending on the individual relationships.

Now try writing a few key words about each mask. If you like, you can even try drawing what a real mask for that aspect of yourself might look like. The goal is to suss out the personality of each one and try to make this part of yourself distinct enough that you can easily identify it.

———

As you're going through these exercises, be honest with yourself if something comes up that really doesn't feel like "you." Sometimes others tell us what they think we should be, and we internalize it. Or we set up false expectations for ourselves that we try to live by. It can be difficult to do this exercise, especially if you find yourself potentially letting go of something you've tended to see as a big part of your self-identity.

Make note of things you wish were a stronger part of who you are or that you'd like to be lesser influences in your life. Later in this chapter I'll discuss how archetypal totemism can help you with self-improvement.

Finally, if at any point you notice animals coming up in your thoughts while you're doing these exercises, jot it down in your journal. They may mean absolutely nothing, but they may also be the first glimmers of archetypal totems stepping forward in conjunction with the parts of yourself you're exploring.

Gather Information

Once you have a good understanding of yourself underway, it's time to turn your attention outward for a while. This step is primarily about researching animals and their totems just to have a large pool of information and ideas to draw from once you start figuring out which totems correspond to which parts of your psyche.

If you've been reading this book cover to cover, you probably noticed that I've mentioned natural history, mythology, and other folklore as source material. In the Archetypal Model of totemism, natural history is the most raw and primal wellspring of symbol fodder out there, and it is also the most objective source. Whether you're observing animals in their habitats or viewing others' footage of them online, this gets you the most direct view of what the animal is and does. Mythology, folklore, and other storytelling are human extrapolations on numerous observations of animals mixed with subjective impressions and biases—and pure creative license. Bullwinkle J. Moose may be far removed from his real-life counterparts, but he's an important marker of what elements of that animal—apparent dimwittedness and random shows of strength, for example—stand out in American pop culture. Even if Bullwinkle isn't meant to be taken particularly seriously, he still demonstrates that animals can be symbols, and the exact symbolism is in the eye of the creator.

Look at some of the animal archetypes that exist in various cultures around the world, to include modern popular media. Bullwinkle is one example of how creative people can get in personifying animal traits. While the animals in cartoons, fairy tales, and even older myths and legends may have been created with human agendas in mind, they are often based on the truths of the animals themselves. When you are assessing the value of fictional animals for your research, look to the behaviors and traits of the real animals on which they're based. Often we are biased toward some animals and against others, particularly in relation to how much we value them and what they can do for us. What do our archetypes say about our relationships to other animals, as well as ourselves? What subjective values do we place on them?

Lisa has always loved wolves. She's always felt bad for the Big Bad Wolf in various fairy tales, though. After all, wolves have to eat something, right? In researching how wolves have been affected by the increase in the human population over millennia, she realizes that often humans want the wild prey animals that wolves need to survive, and so either compete with the wolves for the prey, or kill the wolves to remove competition. Hungry wolves that can't find deer or even rabbits may look to pigs and goats as easy, trapped food. Since the human owners of these livestock don't appreciate sharing them with their lupine neighbors, wolves ended up demonized and turned into quintessential "bad guys," even long after the wolf population has been decimated and factory farming has made wolf predation a lesser concern. Lisa works with the totem Gray Wolf to find ways not only to help the remaining wild wolves, but also to educate people about the misunderstandings. She even finds an opportunity to volunteer her time at a wolf sanctuary near her home.

Totem Animal Dictionaries

A special mention goes to totem animal dictionaries composed largely of the authors' own symbol sets. Dictionaries can offer an introduction to the ways others have built their own totemic symbols systems over time, which readers can then use as templates for their own creations. These resources are a marvelous example of archetypal totemism in action, the idea of one overarching symbol encompassing a set of qualities surrounding a given species.

The common format is to give the animal's name, a few key words of its supposed spiritual meanings, maybe some information about the animal's behavior and mythology, and then the author's own interpretation of the totem's detailed meaning. Sometimes these are acknowledged as being personal to the author, but often they are presented and understood as being more universal, applicable to everyone. Similarly, indigenous totemic lore is frequently offered up as being general-use wisdom regardless of your cultural background (be wary of this). If something in a book doesn't work for you, don't try to shoehorn it into your understanding just because you think you should. Use dictionaries primarily as a guide for structuring your own map, but let the content of that map be your own creation.

It can be challenging to determine what animals to research first. After all, "go and look up stuff about animals" is a pretty vague direction. However, of all the models of totemism, this one has the most freedom for personal choice when it comes to which totems to work with, because it's about your personal symbol system.

You may find as you're doing research that certain animals stand out to you. Make note of them. Also be mindful of any animals that have had a strong presence in your life such as a favorite animal, pets and livestock, or wildlife you encounter repeatedly.

There could also be a specific grouping of animals you find intriguing. Maybe it's particular era of extinct animals like dinosaurs or Paleolithic megafauna. Or, as detailed in the previous chapter, you find yourself really interested in the local wildlife. You might even try working with a sort of spiritual "farm," honoring the pact humans have made with various species we've domesticated, from pigs to pigeons.

If you get really stuck, try turning on the television to Animal Planet or another nature-oriented channel, and watch some shows about animals. Even if no single animal seems especially interesting, you can still get a broad overview of a number of species, especially if you pick shows that feature less common animals.

Take notes as you do your research, or at least create a list of resources you've used. Once you actually start connecting totems to your psyche, it may be helpful to be able to refer back to your research to confirm a spiritual experience's relevance to the physical world. For example, if Pallas Cat seems to be a particularly good match for your preference for introversion, checking back to find out that particular species of feline lives a largely solitary life in isolated mountain ranges would be extra verification. On the other hand, if the animal seems really unfit, such as the solitary Pallas Cat as a potential totem for help with dealing with huge crowds of people, you may want to make a different connection.

Put It Together

There are two parts to this step of the process: building a structure, and arranging totems within that structure. You may find that a structure arises intuitively as you start figuring out which totem speaks to which part of you. If this is not the case, you still have plenty of options.

One good way to learn how to build a map is by exploring the structure of an existing one. Pantheons of deities from numerous cultures draw on various elements of the human experience. The classical Greek pantheon of Olympians (and the Roman pantheon that borrowed very heavily from it) is a good example of a well-rounded grouping. While the deities do not encompass every single role a human may take (and the system is especially limiting for women), the Olympians represented some of what the ancient Greeks considered to be the most important highlights of what it is to be human. The archetypes that are represented are found worldwide throughout recorded history as well—Queen, King, Artisan, Trickster, Warrior, Scholar, Beauty, Maiden, and so forth. Even seemingly simplistic settings such as children's cartoons draw on versions of these archetypes—the Leader, the Strong One, the Scared One, the Wise One, the Pretty One, etc. Over and over they appear in our stories.

This is because we each have a little of all of them within us. All of us have the potential to be leaders or followers, creators or destroyers, independent or collective, playful or serious. Through nature and nurture, some of these potentials come to the fore more often as we develop as human beings, but that doesn't remove the ones that remain primarily dormant. And that dormancy isn't necessarily permanent. Extraordinary circumstances can bring things out in us that we swear could never have been there. Some of the best examples of this are surprising acts of courage where seemingly ordinary, untrained individuals rush into burning buildings or other dangerous situations to save others. The flip side of that is demonstrated by situations such as the Stanford Prison Experiment and the Milgram Experiment, two controversial (and in hindsight unethical) psychological experiments that showed that everyday people can fall victim to pressure from authority and commit heinous acts thereby.

You may already have an affinity for some archetypes. If you haven't really thought about it before, though, the next few exercises are designed to help you identify how some of the archetypes may manifest themselves in your psyche. Feel free to have fun with them, and don't feel that your results are wrong just because they may seem a little silly or far-fetched. What's important is that the symbolism speaks to you. (Making use of Jung's materials, and solid derivations thereof, such as the works of Joseph Campbell and Bill Plotkin, may be quite helpful here.)

The Little Village

In the two Little Village exercises, you can try visiting some of Jung's archetypes, each residing in a different part of a village representing your psyche. Or each part of the village could symbolize a different stage of your life, and so you could take a trip through time, as it were. You can also simply enter, explore freeform without any specific destination, and let the village build itself as you go.

The Little Village, Part I

Get into a comfortable place where you won't be disturbed for at least an hour. Close your eyes, relax, and simply breathe for a few moments, letting the thoughts of the day drift away like leaves on water.

Visualize a little village inside your head. Turn your attention toward it, and shrink your observing self down until you are walking to the edge of this village.

As you walk through this village, you will begin to meet other people there. Talk to them, find out what they do and who they are. Notice what they wear and what they carry, and other features of their appearance and activity.

You might also try asking to speak with specific archetypes, such as "I would like to have an audience with the Queen; would you be so kind as to take me to her?"

and then see what happens. In fact, you may want to start out this entire exercise with a list of specific archetypes you wish to meet. However, be open to the appearance of others, and always allow each archetype to show itself however it sees fit.

Take as much time as you like. When you come out of the meditation, immediately write down as much as you remember. If you feel like there was still more to know, you can always revisit the village again using the same meditation.

———

Who did you meet? If you started with a particular structure such as a pantheon, how well did the villagers match up with what you already knew? Were there any big differences or new archetypes?

What were your experiences like with each of the villagers? Were there any you immediately felt connected to, or others that may have been more difficult to face, even frightening? Did you recognize any of them as ones that commonly appear in your everyday life, or others that may have surprised you by their very presence?

How did the villagers react to you exploring their home? Did any of them act particularly friendly or hostile? Did you find there were places that you were unable to go? Were you able to explore the entire village, or did you have to stop? Why?

If you need to make multiple trips to the village to find out more about who lives there, take your time. It is better to have a thorough understanding of the villagers and what parts of your psyche they represent before you go on to the second Little Village exercise. This gives you a basic structure, the building blocks of yourself.

When you feel you have a good grasp of who's in the village, it's time to connect them with animal totems. Granted, you could just work with the villagers themselves, as they are aspects of yourself. However, adding in the totem animals connects these aspects to the wider world around you. And just as many deities have animals associated with them that illustrate some of their strengths and other traits, so the totem animals can help you to better understand the parts of you they correspond to. Now, let's find out who those totem animals are.

The Little Village, Part II

As before, get comfortable and relaxed, and let the chatter in your mind settle down. Then visualize yourself returning to the village.

Go to each villager you met with previously. Ask each one what his or her favorite animal is. You may have noticed certain animals around them before; these may or may not be their answer. Ask them what they like about the animals they chose and what their relationship to them is like.

If a villager doesn't give you a clear answer, make note of it, and move on to the next. You may need to ask again in a later meditation, or you may need to find them an animal.

The Little Village is just one of many possible structures you can use as a framework for your totemic archetype map. Another one that I like is the Personal Totem Pole Process, a system created by psychologist Eligio Stephen Gallegos. It combines totem animals with the seven primary chakras, as well as some elements of psychotherapy. As I am not formally trained in this process, I can't teach it here; however, Gallegos's book *The Personal Totem Pole* is a thorough overview of how he developed it and how it works. I do know from my own experience that it's a great tool for personal meditative use. If the option sounds viable, I recommend reading his book for yourself.

It may be that you feel ready to just jump right in and work with the animals without little villagers, chakras, or whatnot. That's fine too. Regardless of how you put together your framework, you have a couple of options for populating it with totem animals.

If you feel comfortable and familiar enough with your framework, you can deliberately choose the totem animals associated with your psyche. Look at each aspect of yourself and decide which animal reminds you the most of it as it is now. If you want to actively change that aspect, find a totem that may be able to help you make those improvements.

Write in your journal which totem corresponds to which aspect of yourself and why you chose it. Connect the totem and the information about it to what you know about yourself. Note anything that is a particular strength or challenge, as well as anything that the totem doesn't have in common with you.

Conversely, if you prefer to let your subconscious mind choose the totems for you, here's a guided meditation that may help.

———

First, draw a physical representation of your chosen framework. It might be a series of spokes radiating out from a central point that represents you as a whole. Or it may be plotted against a place you've visited in real life, with different landmarks being the homes of different parts of you. No matter what the framework looks like, do your best to create an image of it.

Next, get into your meditation space, relax, and otherwise prepare to focus. When you're ready, visualize yourself floating over the framework you drew.

Choose one of the locations on the framework that represents an aspect of yourself that you feel pretty comfortable with, and go to it. As you immerse yourself in it, you may find yourself in a particular location such as a wilderness area or a house. Take a little time to explore it and see what's there. As you explore this place, see if any animals show themselves. One in particular may be especially prevalent; pay attention to it, and if you can, talk to it and ask it why it's there.

If no animal shows up on its own, you may need to go searching for it. In the meditation, say "I am ready to meet the totem who lives here." Then look for any signs that point you in the right direction. It may be tracks on the ground or an animal's cry. You may also feel yourself drawn in a particular direction. Whatever it is, follow it, and see who it leads you to. Again, once you find the totem animal of that place, engage it and find out why it above all other animals has become one with that part of you. Then, when you're ready, come back to the waking world, and record your results immediately and in as much detail as possible.

———————

Since you're starting from scratch as opposed to using an established set of archetypes, it's best only to visit one aspect per meditation, so that you can have the most focus on each. If you don't get a clear answer in a meditation, come back out of it, and then try again later. If this happens multiple times with the same aspect, try others, and then go back to that one sometime down the line.

Once you have identified some of the totems of your psyche, you may wish to make a more detailed map of them. The framework you initially used to explore yourself can work, though you may find that the totems have other suggestions, or that your vision of your psyche has changed as you've gone through the series of meditations.

Regardless of what the map has become, having a visual representation of it can help strengthen the associations you've made in it. You might draw out a literal map, showing where the different totems are in proximity to each other within your psyche. Or you could create a mandala depicting the various totems; traditional Hindu and Buddhist mandalas tend to feature abstract, geometric patterns, sometimes with various deities and other spiritual figures worked into the art. However, some Celtic and Celtic-inspired art also features animals "in the round," as it were. Another option is an elaborate coat of arms. You could even draw a series of portraits of yourself, with each portrait depicting you with or even *as* one of the animals. These are just a few ideas for solidifying your psyche's map in your mind.

What might a final map look like? Here's just one potential example using some of my own archetypal totems:

Gray Wolf: My heart, my personal internal emotions, the core of my being; also, connection to the outdoors

Brown Bear: My compassionate self

Red-tailed Hawk: My intellect and direct observation

Red Fox: The strength of gentleness, calm, and change through meditation and focus; also my sense of humor

White-tailed Deer: My dreaming self, the bridge to other levels of consciousness

Mustang: My awareness of my body

I might paint a series of pictures of each one of these totems in different rooms of a house. Brown Bear could be in an office with my various psychology, ecology, and other relevant texts for counseling, while White-tailed Deer might be curled up, asleep and dreaming in the bedroom.

One thing to keep in mind: these are artificial categorizations. When I am doing counseling work, for example, I am not only working with Brown Bear, but I am also engaging my own emotions (Gray Wolf), my training and observation (Red-tailed Hawk), and regulating my emotions with the help of Red Fox. The point is not to separate the self out and see yourself as separate beings, but to know your various parts so as to understand the whole more thoroughly. Think of it as learning the alphabet so you can then form words and communicate fluidly, or learning each card or symbol of a divination set so that you can do more complicated readings later on. It's just that knowing elements of the self is a bit more complex than knowing each letter individually.

Follow the Map

Now that you've gone through all this trouble to create an elaborate representation of your psyche using animal totems to represent different parts of who you are, what do you do with it?

Well, let's start with that old Delphic adage, "Know thyself." A lot of magic and other spiritual practices are aimed at the goal of having a greater understanding of who you are, both to become a better person and to better find your place in the world.

My hope is that in the process of determining the totems you associate with different parts of yourself, you have gotten to know yourself pretty thoroughly, perhaps even learning things you didn't know. However, there's always more to know. We are dynamic, ever-growing beings throughout our lifetimes, stories that are constantly being added to. A good practice is to keep up good communication with your archetypal totems.

One of the best ways to do this is through revisiting them in guided meditation. If you used the Village exercises, for example, you can go back to the village any time to talk to the totems and the parts of yourself they are aligned with. Gallegos's Personal Totem Pole Process includes a "council" with the totems of that system that can be used for continued communication. Additionally, you can use the visual map you made to represent your psyche and the totems in it as a focus for meditation. Try visualizing shrinking yourself down, walking around to different places on the map, and visiting the totems who are there.

What do you talk about once you're there? Here are a few ideas:

Interviewing the Totem

Ask each totem why it showed up in that particular place, and why it's associated with that part of your psyche. This may seem like a simple exercise, but there can be a lot of depth and exploration in making the connections between yourself and the totem. Additionally, since this is a very right-brained activity and you're already starting with a symbol in the form of an animal, the totem may speak in symbols and allegories rather than giving a straight answer, which can bring its own exploration (and frustrations, if the symbols seem confusing!). Still, just as it's enjoyable to simply sit and talk with friends and others whom you care for, it can be nice just to get to know a totem better through casual interaction.

It is also crucial to understand how the totems all work together. Over time, you'll get to know the relationships between the totems—and, thereby, the different parts of yourself. This is especially helpful when you find yourself feeling "of two minds" or conflicted over something. Having a discussion with the totems associated with the conflicted feelings may help you to resolve that conflict. You may also find that certain totems work together a great deal, just as different parts of your psyche interact from moment to moment. Keep using your journal to record what you learn about the different totems and how they work with you (and each other).

Taking Stock of Yourself

Once you have a pretty solid idea of what parts of your psyche a totem corresponds to, look at part of yourself that you might like to change. For example, I have a tendency to worry, probably more than I should. Gray Wolf, my primary totem, is also associated with my heart. So Wolf and I have worked together to help me bring about more calm and steadiness in tough times. Sometimes Wolf has been a little too close to me, though, so I've also asked other totems to come into that part of myself and help out; Red Fox has been very helpful in tempering some of the idiosyncrasies of Wolf (my heart), as one example. And, drawing on bioregional totemism, I have even asked Western Hemlock to help ground the busier animal energies of Gray Wolf and to create more emotional calm.

To do this sort of work, first identify what you'd like to change about yourself. Do you have a bad habit you would like to get rid of? Or is there some skill or talent you'd like to develop further, or even something entirely new to learn? If you have a whole list, that's fine. Just pick one to start.

Next, determine which part of yourself corresponds with what you want to change. Let's say you'd like to get better at meditation, but you find yourself having a hard time sitting still for more than a few minutes. Now, let's also say that the totem that currently represents your ability to focus is Domestic Dog. Dog can be a hard worker, but also (as anyone who has ever taken a dog on a walk knows) can be easily distracted (Squirrel! Another dog! A pile of something stinky and possibly long-dead!).

However, wolves are better focused, in part because they have to be. Dogs are essentially wolves locked in a permanently juvenile mental state. Wolves, on the other hand, have to grow up if they're going to survive because there's no one to give them kibble at the end of a long day of bad hunting. There's still play, but when it comes time to pay attention to business, wolves can do it.

So you may ask Gray Wolf to come in and help you and Dog to learn to focus better. This may include talking with Wolf about strategies for keeping one's focus intact, and also finding out from Dog why focus can be so incredibly difficult. Even if Gray Wolf isn't one of your archetypal totems, you may still create a place for him in your psyche, which is always a work in progress.

Be patient with yourself; change doesn't usually happen overnight. If you're having trouble with making changes or learning new things, you may simply not be ready. Or you could be trying to do too much at once. The best levels of change are those that are difficult enough to present a challenge, but not so tough that you have little to no hope of succeeding. Make sure your goals are realistic, breathe deeply, and continue with that patience.

Also, it's not a complete failure if you revert to your old behavior or lose some skill at some point. During my counseling internship in graduate school I worked with some very deeply addicted women. The facility-wide stance was that relapse was a common part of recovering from addictions, and rather than starting over at square one, a relapse was seen as a learning opportunity and a way to refocus a client's treatment plan. It's also the same way even with less pervasive behaviors. Don't be discouraged if you find yourself slipping back into old patterns or forgetting to practice. Celebrate the successes you have, no matter how small.

Bringing Out Your Best

You can also enlist the help of the totems to bring forth what you have to offer in your everyday life. This isn't so much about changing yourself or developing new skills as it is accentuating your strengths. When I was really getting going as a writer and having my first articles and books published, I worked with Canadian Lynx to really show off and use that part of myself. Having a small stuffed toy lynx on my computer helped me remember that I was already proving myself capable of being a good writer, that I had some publications under my belt, and if I just kept on writing I would get better with practice.

Using your strengths can absolutely be a part of making changes, too. Because my emotional self can sometimes get snappy and snarly like an irritated wolf, I have also brought in some of my counseling skills, my work with Brown Bear, and compassion toward myself and others to tame some of that emotional edge. Again, don't expect miracles (though don't begrudge the occasional one that may occur)! I still have snarly Wolf days where I don't remember how to be more Bear-like myself, but it doesn't take away that Bear strength; it just means I have room to keep trying.

A Caution or Three

Because this can be such "heavy" work, I have a few suggestions that may help you navigate your psyche a little more safely.

Not a Substitute

If you are currently receiving mental health counseling or similar professional care, you may wish to talk to your therapist about potentially integrating this totemic work with your care. If you are uncertain about how to explain what you're trying to do spiritually, you may consider showing your therapist this chapter. Additionally, Gallegos himself is a psychotherapist who created the Personal Totem Pole Process as a tool for professional therapeutic use. If you happen to have his book, *The Personal Totem Pole*, it may also be a useful resource.

As a counselor myself, I like when clients offer me more information to help me better understand them and be of more help. While in the past many therapists avoided integrating spirituality into therapy, preferring instead to refer clients to their spiritual clergy, more and more therapists are approaching a client's spirituality as an integral part of who the client is. Additionally, better diversity training means that more therapists are able to approach a variety of religious, spiritual, and cultural backgrounds in their clients in a sensitive, nonjudgmental manner.

Ground Yourself

One thing you want to be very aware of is that it is possible to get entangled in runaway flights of fantasy and imagination instead of basing your understanding of archetypal totems in yourself. It's a good idea to reality-check yourself on a regular basis when doing this work. Keep in mind that these totems are representing parts of your psyche. If something a totem is saying or doing sounds really uncharacteristic for you, take a step back and figure out whether you're letting your imagination, wishful thinking, or some other distraction get you carried away from the work's original focus.

Additionally, be wary of externalizing the totems too much in this model. Although the totems within you are connected to the overarching totems outside of you, whether you see them as shared symbols or as actual independent beings, your internal totems are very much composed of parts of you. While some projection of yourself into the world is fine, be careful that you aren't losing the connection to yourself. This is primarily an internal model of totemism, and it needs to stay mainly within your own psyche.

What does this disconnection look like? You may start feeling yourself "fragmenting" into more than one person. Note that this is not automatically a sign of something like dissociative identity disorder (formerly multiple personality disorder), with "split personalities." But if you start thinking of yourself as, for example, a distinct Human self and Bear self to the point where you can't control when the Bear comes out, it may be time to take a break from this sort of totemic work for a while. Even deliberate shapeshifting magic is carefully controlled to maintain balance. The goal of all this is to have a stronger understanding of the whole self by getting to know the individual pieces of what makes you *you*, and also understanding that the whole is greater than the sum of all the parts. Again, think of it like learning the letters of the alphabet or the parts of an engine.

Animals Buried in Archetypes

If we are to learn from the totems, it is crucial that we keep a good focus on their physical children. Humans are all too good at passing judgment on other beings, human and otherwise, and sometimes the negative stereotypes we make about animals have caused us to unfairly persecute them. Wolves, for examples, have been hunted perhaps more vigorously than other large predators because of the strong bias against them and the tales demonizing them in European and other cultures.

This behavior is obviously detrimental to the animals, and these biases and judgments are also harmful to us. It's hard for us to maintain connections with other beings, whether on a spiritual level or not, when our first action is to try to figure out how to kill them, especially when we feel hostile toward them (as opposed to relatively neutral in the case of animals we kill for food). We can still hunt and fish and farm, but doing so with respect as the first priority furthers one's spiritual efforts in this regard. Additionally, when we are empathetic toward an animal we intend to kill, we tend to try to be more humane and quick about the death, and not to kill unnecessarily.

It is important, then, to sometimes take the animals as they are without our biases, stories, and overlays of myth and judgment. They are not created for us; they simply exist as we do. They are their own as we are our own. Beyond that, it is us laying our burdens upon them.

Is It Helping?

This is work meant to benefit you and others, not harm you. If at any time a totem is telling you to do something detrimental to yourself or to others, or if you otherwise feel that this work is leading you into dangerous territory, stop this work immediately. If you know other totemists, shamanic practitioners, or Neopagan folk whom you trust, you may want to ask them for their advice on the spiritual end of things. You also might assess the possibility that you may need to seek professional mental health counseling if you feel that this work is touching on difficult territory or changing you for the worse.

Six

Totemic Combinations

I've spent the past few chapters offering you some alternative models of totemism to the usual quasi-shamanic, indigenous-inspired model found in many existing books on the subject. Don't feel that you have to stick with an existing model, though; my own work with animal totems was self-taught and came through a lot of trial and error working directly with the totems themselves. And if you find some parts of what I've discussed here helpful, but other parts not so much, take what's working for you and leave the rest.

There are a couple of options I'm going to discuss. One is to combine two or three of the models in the previous chapters. Given that all three of them were drawn from my own practice, I can say from experience that they can and do play well together. However, we're going to be going in two different directions—I drew three different models out of my single practice, while you're going to be making one path for yourself out of the elements of those three models. Just as two different painters can be given identical sets of watercolors but won't make the exact same painting, I don't expect your combination of these varying models to necessarily resemble my own.

The other option is to combine totemism with other spiritual and magical systems. Let's say you already have a spiritual or magical path that you've been following. Maybe you're a Qabalist wishing to be more immersed in Malkuth through the experiences of other living beings and their archetypal counterparts. Or you could be a heathen with an interest in the sacred animals of various Germanic cultures. You might even be like I was when I got started, one of many Wicca-flavored Neopagans with no specific tradition but an interest in eclecticism. And yes, it is possible to be part of a nonpagan religion such as a liberal denomination of Christianity and still work with animal totems. Even someone who is theologically an agnostic or atheist can still work with totems on a symbolic and metaphorical level.

There is a third option I will not get into here: creating an entire totemic model from scratch. This is a broad and involved process that can't be neatly fit into a single chapter. A previous book of mine, *DIY Totemism: Your Personal Guide to Animal Totems*, is a complete manual on developing your own relationships with the totems and building a framework to work with them from the ground up. Rather than repeating a lot of material from that in an insufficient number of pages, I will simply recommend that title to those of you who are curious about taking that route.

Combining Models of Totemism

At this point I have introduced you to three different models of animal totemism. Each has its own focus:

- *The Correspondences Model* makes connections among totem animals, directions, seasons, elements, and other external correspondences. Good for those who like to find similarities among various systems of symbols and qualities.

- *The Bioregional Model* helps you to get to know your immediate environment more thoroughly and understand your place in it. Excellent for those who may be feeling disconnected from the rest of the world, especially its nonhuman portions.

- *The Archetypal Model* is intimately concerned with your internal landscape, and a nice choice for those who live by the motto "know thyself."

It would be impossible for me to completely describe the interplay of these different models in my own practice, but allow me to give a small taste. I feel that totems are both internal and external beings; they are bridges not only between their respective species and the rest of the world (to include humans and other animals), but also by their very natures they are "made of" both the qualities of external animals, and our internal individual and collective thoughts and ideas about those animals.

Think of "internal" and "external" as a continuum. We are never really on one end or the other; instead, we constantly move back and forth as needed. For example, if I am calling on the totems of the directions in a ritual, I use my body as a conduit for the totems to travel into my ritual space. They connect to that part of me that resonates with them and what they need, and for a brief moment they use that to enter into the ritual space I have created with intent. However, they remain primarily external beings, and I work with them as such.

However, if I happen to be meditating with a totem on some internal work I'm doing, I'm primarily going to be seeing that totem as a part of who I am. I don't take a strict Jungian perspective and see them as only internal, but I've definitely moved along more toward that end of the continuum. I might be working with Brown Bear to improve my ability to be a good counselor, and so most of what I'm focusing on are my own abilities and limitations. If I decide to come out of the meditation and do a ritual with Brown Bear to help me attract the best clients for me to work with right now (a lot of this also has to do with the urban environment I am a part of), I might also enlist the help of Scrub Jay as a local connection. Additionally, my focus is now more balanced between internal and external, so I am working with both the totems within and the totems as independent beings.

When you're combining two or all three models of totemism, be aware of the internal/external balance of each one and how they affect each other. I've just described how my sense of whether a totem I'm working with is inside me or outside me me can shift from situation to situation, such as in the example where I work with Brown Bear internally and Scrub Jay externally for the same basic purpose. But Brown Bear can also exist outside of me, and I can do internal work with Scrub Jay, too. In order to work with all of these models, you may need to look at totems as having multiple natures or existences, some of which are independent of human thought and feeling, some that are entirely based in our psyches—and all points in between.

Before you decide how much of each model to draw from, it's a good idea to figure out how you see totems, whether you see them as only internal or external, or whether you're okay with some combination thereof. If you've already tried out the models individually and gotten a feel for them, which one(s) appeal the most to you?

What do you feel totems are—internal, external, or both? What feels right to you?

———————

The next few pages are dedicated to a few ideas for combining the models once you've decided which ones you want to put together.

Correspondences and Bioregional

Correspondences are good ways of creating and making use of patterns, and nature is full of patterns. Correspondences are a way we apply subjective value to something. When combing these two models, be careful not to lose sight of the reality of the animals and other beings as themselves, free of our human judgments. Connect your personal feelings and experiences with the totems and their children with the physical and independent realities of the animals themselves. It's a good thing if you can look at a garter snake and be inspired to renew yourself through a symbolic shedding of skin and better yourself that way. But also remember that the snake doesn't shed its skin for you, and it would continue to do so whether you noticed or not.

- You can limit your directional animals to only those found in your bioregion. However, you can also expand on this further by linking the directions to entire surrounding bioregions, ecosystems, or similar physically demarcated natural spaces as a basis for your totemic practice. For example, just to the north of Portland where I live is the Columbia River, a formidable ecosystem in and of itself. West of the city there is ample farmland and some remaining wetlands; the southern area is similar. East there are the Cascades, and farther beyond that the high sagebrush desert. So I could do work with each one of those bioregions/ecosystems and find a representative totem animal for each, and those would also be my directional totems.

· Instead of working with directions, work with elements instead. What are the earthy animals in your bioregion—which ones live in or close to the ground? Who is in the water? Which animals fly through the air? What animals need the sun and the heat the most to survive? Are there animals that have more abstract connections to the elements (such as through alchemical or other symbolism) that also inhabit your bioregion?

· Try working with systems of correspondence other than the elements or directions. If you were to create a tarot deck based in your bioregion, what animals would be associated with each of the cards? What about the Norse or Anglo-Saxon runes, or the Celtic ogham?

· Create correspondences based on your observations
  of the relationships between the animals and other
  beings in your bioregion. Meditate, for example,
  on the relationship between a red-tailed hawk and
  a field mouse. To many people, the hawk is "bad"
  because it kills. Yet mice and other small animals
  are an integral part of the ecosystem because they
  provide food; they have numerous offspring because
  so many of them die before reproducing, and their
  lifespans are short. Many large predator species
  would not exist without the small prey. So perhaps
  Field Mouse may be associated with strength
  through sacrifice; what else is associated with that
  idea? Are there deities, rituals, or concepts such as
  humility or necessity associated with sacrifice that
  can also be connected to Field Mouse? Are there
  places in your bioregion that have been the site of
  sacrifices of varying sorts, including altruistic ones?

Bioregional and Archetypal

Working with these two models can be a great way to connect the external world to the deepest parts of the self. In
the Western world, we are often trained to be quite cerebral and virtual in our approach to what's around us as
well as what's within. Rooting ourselves in the place we
live reminds us that we do not exist as independent au-

tomatons but as integral parts of systems that include the psychological level.

When we look at the Shadow self, for example, we are reminded of our primal, mammalian, reptilian, and older ancestors whose basic behaviors may still be mirrored in our own. Today we may fear abstract things like being audited for taxes or not being able to pay the rent, but the process of feeling fear and the insecurity about one's own safety and stability in these examples hearken back to our ancestors' fears of starvation and death. Our Shadow may cause us to act out in fear in ways that are much older than our human species, and remembering that we are animals in an ecosystem can help us understand our Shadow as well as other deeply ingrained archetypes.

Working with bioregional totems can help us to further remember how to be an animal in the home we're in, and why we feel and act the way we do. Scrub Jay has helped me to deal with some of the stressors of living in the city, so when I start to feel crowded and want to lash out because of it, instead of falling prey to my Shadow I can talk to Scrub Jay about how his children have adapted to the changes humans have wrought on their native landscape, and how I can also adapt to the same.

- Look at the stages of your life you've already completed. Are there particular places in your bioregion that the "you" in each stage might prefer? If you've lived in the same bioregion all your life, did you have specific places that were important to you at each stage? Try mapping your psyche out on your local bioregion; is there a place for every piece of yourself? What place or landmark in your bioregion might you associate with wholeness and completion (Jung's Self)? Is there perhaps a dangerous waterway, such as a whitewater or an ocean undertow, that could be the Shadow?

· You might even leave small, ecofriendly but relatively permanent symbols of the parts of your psyche at the places in the bioregion they correspond to as a way of strengthening the connection. For example, let's say you're exploring your psyche with a bioregional map. In your meditation, you go to a small wooded area in a public park not too far from home, and there you find a statue representing the Child archetype at play. You might leave a small memento in that spot in the corresponding location in the physical world. Make sure it's not something you'd be sad to lose if some other explorer happened to find it.

· You can also look at the age of the places themselves; a newly restored wetland may "feel" younger than a protected old-growth forest. These may also be connected to stages of your life. This doesn't always have to be a young place with a young self, however.

A younger self may feel more comfortable in a protective cave or cleanly mowed yard, while an older, more adventurous self may look to more risk and exploration, climbing mountains or taking on challenging surf or whitewater rapids.

· If you did the Little Village or other archetype meditation exercises, did any of the archetypes show up in particular types of ecosystem? You might also try going back to the Village or other map and asking each of the archetypes if there is a special place in your bioregion they might like to visit with you or be associated with.

Archetypal and Correspondences

Just as we can use correspondences as a language to speak about the outer landscape, we can also use them to work with the inner landscape. In fact, correspondences and archetypes are very closely related to each other; correspondences are one way in which we project our biases onto the world around us, and they often come from the same sorts of deep impulses that birth archetypes.

If this combination of models appeals to you, I would again strongly recommend Whitcomb's *The Magician's Reflection* as it is specifically about archetypes and correspondences. It would be a highly valuable resource for your research.

· How can you connect the outer correspondences with your inner archetypes? One way might be taking Jung's five classic archetypes and assigning them to the four cardinal directions, plus center. The true, integrated Self could be in the center, while the deep, dark Shadow lies in the caves of the north where there is fear but also much quiet wisdom. The Animus might rise in the east with the sun, while the Anima swims in cool waters to the west, both balancing each other. And the ever-shifting Persona dances in southern flames, transforming as needed. Who are the totem animals who can help you to better know these parts of yourself and the symbolic places in which they live?

· Or work from the other direction: take your inner archetypes and do more research into the correspondences associated with them, then find totems to match. What are qualities that have traditionally been associated with the Great Mother? What traits have been found in Mother figures in cultures around the world? Are there any animals that have been associated with these goddesses and other women? What about traits and animal symbols of other archetypes?

· As you're working with the totems associated with your archetypes, are there any traits you don't share with the totems? Does this have any effect on your work with them? For example, let's say you're working with your inner Trickster, who tends to be rather playful, and is connected to Coyote. Yet in reading some of the stories traditionally told about Coyote, at times there's an element of maliciousness you don't resonate with, even at your most tricksy. What does it mean? Is Coyote still a good fit, or is there a totem who might match you better in that respect? Are there reasons Coyote may be a less kind Trickster than you are, but you still choose to work with this part of yourself?

All Three Models (Correspondences, Bioregional, and Archetypal)

If there are many ways to combine two models together, there are even more ways to combine all three! I'll offer a few starting points here, but understand that these combinations aren't like recipes where there are set amounts of each ingredient. Instead, think of each model as a set of paints, each contributing some colors that can be added to a canvas in varying amounts and patterns, painted over, and so forth.

Joshua tends to be a very cerebral person, "lost in his head" a good deal of the time. He does a lot of self-reflection and is very knowledgeable about his own motivations for doing things. However, he finds himself often feeling detached from the rest of the world, not just other people, but also not leaving his home as often as he would like. He starts doing research on animals in his area, and finds some he can relate to as a quiet, introverted person. For example, he has connected strongly to Box Turtle as a safe protector of his own inner child who feels the fear of the unknown and the dangerous. Box Turtle empathizes with Joshua's need to carry his home with him and wanting to stay close to where he feels safe. However, she also points out to Joshua that a strong shell can help keep one safe when venturing out into the world. She convinces him to start exploring a small wetland near his home where he meets not only box turtles waddling their way through the grass, but also other people enjoying the scenery, walking their dogs, going for jogs, and so forth. He carries this growing shell from Box Turtle in his center, and over time he explores other areas of his home territory, finding natural places in each of the four cardinal directions he can visit. He learns from the totems there how to further his explorations into the world, as well as meeting other people and becoming more comfortable with being social.

Helen enjoys the outdoors, and is an avid hiker, kayaker, and runner. She also does nature photography focusing on animals as a creative hobby. She has been feeling the need for more spirituality in her life, like there may be more out there than just what she can find with her physical senses.

She feels especially attracted to Douglas squirrels, whose energetic acrobatics and curious chittering never fail to cheer her up when she's out in the woods. She starts collecting photos and other images of Douglas squirrels, and soon a small shelf is covered in them. She writes about the little animals and how they symbolize the joy and freedom she feels whenever she gets to be outdoors. In exploring these thoughts further, she remembers that sunrise is her favorite time of the day, so she moves the images over to the east side of her home. Every time she walks by their new shelf, she feels a boost of happiness, just like when she was a child first exploring the outdoors with her family. When talking to a friend about her new spiritual pursuits, she finds out about animal totemism and Jung's archetypes, namely the Child archetype that seems so appropriate. Perhaps, she thinks, Douglas Squirrel may be a good first totem for her to talk to about this important part of her life.

I've offered you some examples of how you can combine the various models, but don't feel those are your only options. If you decide to make your own unique combinations, I would again recommend working with each one individually for a while, just to get a good familiarity with what each has to offer. Keep using your journal to take notes, though, because you may find that as you work with one model, there may be experiences or insights you have that may be very relevant to another model as well.

Combining Totemism and Other Systems

The actual process of combining animal totemism and another path may be as simple as calling upon animal totems at the directions instead of (or along with) watchtowers, angels, or whatever other being you associate with each quarter. Many people wish to take it further, which brings up several factors.

One consideration is rigidity versus flexibility. There is a tendency in a lot of religions and spiritual paths to have a certain section of the group that is very oriented toward tradition and doing things "right." In and of itself, this is not a bad thing; keeping track of the roots of a spiritual path is an important part of preserving its legacy into the future. It also allows us to track how that spirituality evolves over time, as no path is without change, no matter how traditional.

What does this mean for you? The first thing you need to do is to determine how much of a traditionalist you are—or aren't. Do you feel that adding totemism to your existing practice will change it enough that you'll essentially be following a different path? Or are you of the mind that animal totems are a natural extension of what you're already doing?

Getting the opinions of others can be helpful in getting alternate ideas and perspectives you might not have thought of before. In fact, other people in your spiritual community may have very constructive advice as to how to work with animals and totems within your path. Ultimately, however, you're the one who has to walk your path, so it's up to you to determine what to do with all the information and advice you receive. Decisions may include whether you think adding totemism to your existing path is a good idea or a separate practice.

On a side note, there's a common idea that one *must* only adhere to one faith or practice. You're either *only* a shamanic practitioner, *only* a Wiccan, or *only* a Druid, etc. What I and others have found in practice multiple times is that it's quite possible to maintain more than one spiritual or magical path at once. You don't have to blend them, mind you. Rather, they can be maintained as separate practices. I know people who have been called on by deities from very disparate cultures, and they do their best to practice each religion associated with those deities. So a person might be a Celtic reconstructionist and do his or her best to practice the religion of a particular Celtic culture or set of cultures but also maintain a dedication to one of the orisha in Vodou, perhaps keeping a head of Eleggua by the front door and "feeding" and caring for it as prescribed.

If you believe that totemism can be added into your current path with little to no trouble, the next thing you'll want to do is to look at how animals already figure into your path in general. If you follow a religion or spirituality that has a particular cultural mythos associated with it, are there stories about animals, and how are they portrayed?

Are there any sacred animals in your path? Do the deities ever show up in animal form or have animals associated with them? Are there already totems or totem-like beings there? What's the relationship of your spirituality to the natural world in general? Are animals seen as beneficial, malevolent, neutral, or resources to be used by humans?

If there are already symbolic or totemic animals in your path, this may be a good framework for you to use to add totemism to your practice. Find out why they're integral to that path, and why the people who created the path in the first place favored them. Do research on this subject using books and other resources, and try talking to the relevant totems as well. If you follow a Celtic-inspired path, you might try researching the importance of animals like wild boars, cattle, and hounds to Celtic cultures, and also talk to the totems European Boar, Domestic Cow, and Domestic Dog to determine how these and other totems may be able to work with you in your path.

Also find out whether there are any beliefs, rituals, and other practices associated with the animals. Is there a taboo on eating certain animals' flesh, such as the Hindu prohibition on beef, or certain rites to be performed after the animals is killed or before the meat can be eaten? Are certain animals shown in a negative light, perhaps even to be avoided? Are there any yearly celebrations associated with animals?

The next big question: how realistic is it for you to take on these beliefs and practices? You're going to need to determine how much of a traditionalist to be—or not. If you decide to pick and choose which you'll follow and which really aren't for you, there may be people who protest and say "You're not doing it right!" I am of the mind, myself, that what *works* for a person is what's most right for them, whether that involves being a full-on traditionalist or an adventurous eclectic.

What if there are no animals associated with your path, or you don't really connect with the ones that are there? That's where you may need to get a little more creative. Start by thinking about any systems of correspondences—or connections between related, parallel concepts—in your path. If you came up with some correspondences while working through the Correspondences Model chapter of this book, review them and see how they've worked for you so far.

Did you find any animals associated with certain directions, elements, colors, practices, deities, spirits, etc. that you work with in your path? If not, are there any animals that you personally associate with these correspondences? Again, the Correspondences Model chapter may come in handy; make use of the guided meditations there to seek out totems for each correspondence. For example, if crystals and other stones are a big part of your practice, you may try holding one particular type of stone in your hand, and then visualize meeting the spirit of the stone and seeing if it suggests a particular animal to you.

Also, determine if any of the models I discussed appeals to you and might mesh well with your path. If you follow a nature-based spirituality, the Bioregional Model might be right up your alley. On the other hand, if your path values the power of myth, metaphor, and transformative ritual, the Archetypal Model of totemism may be a good fit.

You may need to create additional practices surrounding the totems if convenient rites made for animal spirits don't already exist in your path. Are there rituals for other spiritual beings in your path, and if so, can you adapt them for totemic use in part or in whole? The practice of calling on totems at the quarters/directions is one simple example. If your path tends to make use of elaborate symbols and invocations for spirits to join a ritual, you may wish to create these for the individual totems you'll be working with as well.

The totems themselves may have suggestions. They may let you know what's working (or not working) and even come up with ideas of their own. If you feel these will fit into your practice, give them a try; if you feel there's a conflict, bring this up with the totems and see what you can work out.

The totems may also refuse certain types of rituals and other practices. In my own experience, totems tend to be relatively easygoing but also quite independent, and I've found they tend to respond best to politeness and invitations rather than demands and coercion. I'm not particularly likely to try to use a classic Goetic invocation to call upon a totem, with its threats and bindings. After all, totems are animals like us, and a trapped animal is more likely to fight or attempt to escape than to be cooperative. Keep the totems' nature in mind as much as the parameters of your chosen path.

Above all, give it some time. Combining animal totemism with various spiritual and magical paths, especially ones that didn't originally have much to do with animals in the first place, can be a challenge. You may need to adjust your practice a good bit to accommodate the totems, and you may even end up just making totemism a separate practice if it isn't a good fit.

Seven

Other Work with Animal Totems

This chapter is a collection of additional ideas and activities you can use to work with and strengthen your connection to the totems. Throughout this book I've tried to offer a variety of exercises that go beyond finding out what your totem is. For some people, just knowing the totem is enough, and any lessons that may follow occur organically and intuitively. However, as with any spiritual or magical practice, we can also be more proactive in our work with the spirits we connect with, and totemism can be much more than just having the simple presence of

totems in our lives. I've touched on some of these practices in previous chapters, but feel free to integrate these
into your practice as you see fit, regardless of what model
you use.

The Children of the Totems

I often refer to living animals as the totems' children,
though in a way the totems are the animals' children, as the
natural history of animals is crucial to totemic knowledge.
Some people connect most strongly to totems through
living physical animals, and in fact there are those who
were introduced to their totems through those interac-
tions. As you may recall, my relationship with Gray Wolf
was sparked by my imaginative observation of the family
dog when I was a young child.

Now, not every animal you encounter is going to be
indicative of a totemic presence. Sometimes a hawk is
just a hawk. However, if you suspect that the recent appearance of an animal in your everyday life has totemic
significance, your best bet is to use a guided meditation
to visit the totem of that species to verify whether or not
that significance is there.

> *Megan has been seeing a lot of butterflies around as of late,*
> *particularly black swallowtails. She has butterflies in her*
> *garden every year, but the unusual appearance of these enor-*
> *mous black-winged butterflies has her curious as to whether*

it has any spiritual significance. While sitting out in her garden on a sunny day, she uses guided meditation to travel to a beautiful field of flowers where the totem Black Swallowtail rests on a particularly large sunflower. In speaking with the totem, Megan discovers that in conjunction with a particularly healthy population of these butterflies, it is a good time for her to explore her own visibility. She has been feeling rather isolated in her life, and hasn't been taking such good care of herself. With Black Swallowtail's guidance, she takes the time to go through her wardrobe and rediscover some of her favorite outfits. She also remembers that she hasn't been mountain biking in ages, something she used to enjoy on her own and with friends. She makes plans with some of her biking buddies to hit the trail again, and they decide to make a regular occasion of it.

Conversely, a person may use contact with the physical counterparts of a totem to better get to know that totem. One way that you can give back to your totem is by caring for its physical children. This may involve activities like rescuing abused pets, volunteering at a wildlife sanctuary, or giving funds to nonprofit groups that work to save wild creatures and their habitats.

It's crucial to be aware of what effect physical interaction has on the animals themselves. If your totem is Cougar, even if it is technically legal where you live to have a pet cougar in your home, this may end up being a disaster. Even hand-raised wild animals are still wild, and very few people have the training, time, room—and, of course, money—to be able to properly care for any exotic pet, let alone a cute little kitten that will grow up into a large, dangerous cat weighing several hundred pounds.

Even if your totem's counterpart is a smaller exotic animal that may seem easier to care for, the animal's welfare should come first. People often keep small rodents and even ferrets in little clear plastic boxes with a few air holes, or small cages. Yet these animals benefit from having greater run of the home, whether in a plastic hamster ball for small critters or free-roaming for ferrets. There are many more common mistakes people can make in their care, such as poor-quality, cheap food, insufficient veterinary care, or lack of education in the animals' social needs.

If you are in a situation where your totem's physical children are well-adapted to regular human contact (like domestic animals), and if you are in a position to properly care for such an animal, you may find that the relationship with the pet can also enhance your work with the totem. People often get along well with the animals associated with their totems, and the simple interaction can be beneficial all around.

The presence of the physical animal may also invite the totem to be there as well. If it won't harm the animal, you can include it in your meditations with the totem and strengthen the connection. You may also find that the totem manifests through the animal sometimes; the best way to describe this phenomenon is that you can "feel" the totem has arrived. The animal may even act differently, for example being calm when normally it is quite energetic. (You should, of course, rule out other reasons for the inactivity such as illness or the fact that even the most active animal needs a break sometimes.)

Even if you can't have the appropriate animal at home, you may be able to visit well-maintained zoos or sanctuaries. Failing that, simply learning about the animal can help facilitate connection with the totem. And anything you can do to maintain the presence of the living animals in this world can be a huge benefit to the totem as well as the animals; in my experience one of the things that a totem may appreciate the most is help for its children. Whether volunteering time at a wildlife sanctuary, giving money to efforts to preserve wildlife and habitat, or supporting laws that protect animals, every effort you can make does make a difference. Appendix A includes a list of animal-based nonprofit organizations that may be of interest.

More Live and Not-So-Live Ones

While live animals may be appealing to many, dead animals are a bit more controversial. American culture in particular doesn't deal with death very well, and recent efforts by animal rights activists to increase awareness of animal abuse often include shaming anyone who eats meat, wears fur or leather, or otherwise makes use of animal remains.

Before we proceed further, I want to emphasize very strongly that *you* need to make your own boundaries here, no matter what I or anyone else tell you. While I will be discussing how to incorporate animal remains into totemic work, you are in no way obligated to do the same—you are entitled to think this entire section is gross and skip it if you prefer. If you think all this stuff is right up your alley, read on!

First, I want to introduce my working theory about spirits and animal remains. When an animal dies, what we might consider the soul of the animal departs and goes to wherever it's going to go next. However, there remains (no pun intended) a sort of "residue" or "haunt," a remnant of the once-living animal's energy and personality, soaked into the remains. If the body is left to decay, this dissipates, but if the remains are preserved, such as with tanned hides, or bones kept on a shelf, these spiritual "remains" also stay intact. Though they're found in all parts of the animal, I often refer to them collectively as "skin spirits."

Eating Your Totem

The spirits are also found in meat, eggs, and other animal products we eat. We are what we eat, and this animal essence becomes a part of us. This is why in some cultures instead of avoiding eating one's totem animal, the physical animal is instead deliberately hunted down and eaten as part of a rite of passage; consuming the animal gives the person its strength, or so the theory goes.

In fact, let's start with consumable animal parts since they'll be relevant to more people. Here in the U.S., the animals most commonly eaten are domestic, and are limited to just a few—cows, pigs, chickens, turkeys, and to a somewhat lesser extent sheep, goats, and a few other species. Wild animals also make it onto American plates, usually seafood, but some people hunt deer, elk, bears, and other game that ends up eaten.

With few exceptions, most animals cannot or will not be eaten, either due to legalities, accessibility, or simple bad taste, so there's a good chance you couldn't eat your totem's physical counterparts even if you wanted to. However, you can work with the totems of the animals you do eat to be a healthier eater on a spiritual level.

The sad fact is that most of the commercially produced meat and other animal-based foods in the U. S. are from factory-farmed animals who were raised in horrible conditions and killed in even worse ones. And while free-range meats and such are becoming more available, for many people they're still not quite affordable in the average American omnivore's diet, which tends to be pretty meat-heavy.

If you are an omnivore, try talking to the totem of the animals you tend to eat to ask them what you can do to be more mindful of the relationship you have with the animals themselves, as well as the industry they come from. Totems such as Domestic Cow and Domestic Chicken don't get nearly as much attention as they ought to because they aren't flashy or impressive, and many people think of their physical children as stupid or dirty. Why have Cow as a totem when you can have Elk? And yet Cow is so much more relevant to our experience, not only as provider of food, but also as a reflection of what our culture has become through technology and apathy.

Dennis grew up on a farm, but as an adult has spent many years living in a city. He still eats meat, and tries to buy free-range whenever he can. Still, he wants to do more to honor the animals who die to feed him. The next time Dennis buys a free-range chicken, he calls on the totem Chicken to guide him through a ritual as he prepares to cook it. He reverently handles the chicken as though it were the sacred remains of a loved one, remembering in every moment that this was once a living, breathing animal until just a day or two ago. He asks Chicken to watch over the spirit of the bird as it is released from the body. And later, as he consumes the meat, he thinks of how molecules from it that are becoming a part of his body were once a part of the chicken, and before that the grass and insects and other things the chicken ate, continuing in their ongoing cycle from being to being.

Domestic Totems

Domestic totems can also help you to change your relationship to the animals you eat in addition to the molecules and energy that become part of you. Our bodies are entirely made of food we've eaten, and our spirits are likewise nourished. By talking to these totems, you can learn what they have to teach, and remember those lessons when you eat meat and other animal-based foods. You can also create rituals to honor the animals themselves, and handle and prepare their remains in a respectful manner that acknowledges the gravity of taking that life into your own body, as well as consciously absorbing the spirit of the animal through eating and digestion.[23]

The domestic totems may have specific restrictions or other requests, such as buying free-range meat or eggs when you can afford it, or educating yourself on the factory farming process so you are at least aware of what you're buying. Do your best to honor these within your means, but be realistic about what you are and aren't able or willing to do.

Not all domestic totems are of animals that we eat, however. Many of us live with cats or dogs, as well as smaller animals such as rats and other rodents, reptiles and

---

23. And yes, the very same principles do apply to plants and their totems as well. A very dear friend of mine, Paleo, has done a good bit of work with "kitchen totems," and even described some of this work in an essay called "Kitchen Animism," in my anthology *Engaging the Spirit World: Shamanism, Totemism, and Other Animistic Practices.*

amphibians, fish, and even spiders and other invertebrates. Others may even have horses, pigs, cows, and poultry as dedicated pets. While we may not rely on these animals for food, we gain the benefit of their company, and we have a responsibility to them in a way that we do not to wild creatures, as domestic animals depend on us to survive.

There's a lot to learn from the totems of these animals, as well. Dog can teach us about loyalty and connection, even at the cost of one's own health and safety, as well as not taking the sacrifices of others for granted. Cat, on the other hand, is a good reminder of the wild roots of our companions, and that just like us, they exhibit physiology and behaviors that were developed by countless wild ancestors.

Anna has always had parrots, ever since she was very young. She enjoys having these colorful, intelligent birds around, and one of her current feathered companions is an African gray parrot. So it was no surprise when African Gray Parrot arrived in her meditation when she was exploring animal totemism. Parrot reminded her of the responsibility of only buying captive-bred birds, as wild populations have been significantly reduced by the illegal pet trade. Their conversation also helps her to think more about how well she cares for her birds. Although she has done a lot of book research and spoken to her vet a good deal, she decides to reach out to other parrot owners to find

out if there are ways she can make her own birds' lives in
her home even better.

Critter Bits

Less common a practice overall, but perhaps one that is
much more near and dear to my heart, is the work with
preserved animal remains such as leather, fur, and feathers. Since the mid-1990s I've worked with these remains
in ritual and artwork; in fact, this is how I discovered the
existence of skin spirits in the first place.

One of the biggest reasons for this work I do is to
give the remains (which I very often get secondhand) and
skin spirits a better "afterlife" than being a trophy on the
wall, a rug on the floor, or a coat in the closet for that
matter. Skin spirits are also a good connection to the totems themselves, and when I work with these spirits I
often feel the presence of their respective totems.

There are a number of ways you can do the same. Some
people simply collect dead things. They may have a collection of skulls hanging on the wall, hides draped over the
bed, shelves of bones, and so forth. Some of these may have
particular spiritual significance, included as part of an altar
or shrine or as individual ritual tools.

If you choose to go this route, be aware of both ethi-
cal and legal issues surrounding possessing and purchas-
ing animal parts. Some people only collect naturally shed
antlers, molted feathers, and the like. Others will allow

themselves secondhand remains such as old fur, leather coats, and reclaimed taxidermy. If you're going to purchase "new" remains, particularly online, be very careful about your sources, and make sure that you're not inadvertently supporting poachers. Also, if you're curious about legalities, at least in the United States, I maintain a collection of links to information about international, federal, and state laws surrounding animal parts in this country at http://www.thegreenwolf.com/partslaws.html.

Instead of collecting new-to-you things, you may wish to incorporate sacredness to everyday animal parts you already have. For example, most people don't think of the totemic Cow when wearing a leather bomber jacket, or Mink when using mink oil to condition that leather. Yet by treating these seemingly everyday things as sacred remains, we can recapture reverence for them and their totems.

Again, I don't wish to be redundant; I have dedicated an entire book, *Skin Spirits: The Spiritual and Magical Use of Animal Parts*, to this topic, so if these few paragraphs have piqued your interest, you may find it a good resource. Additionally, I speak a good deal about my work with the skin spirits at my blog at http://therioshamanism.com.

Alison's great aunt recently passed away, leaving her a vintage mink stole made of several mink hides in her will. Alison has never owned any fur before, but she wants to keep the mink as a memory of her relative. Still, she feels sad about these animals having lost their lives just to become a fashion accessory, and so she places them on her nature altar. One day as she is meditating, she imagines that there are six little minks bouncing around her, one for each of the skins in the stole. She tells them they can have free run of the house, for it is a safe place for them, but they're always welcome to return to the shelter of the altar. From then on, she often "sees" a little flash of brown fur out of the corner of her eye or has the occasional sighting of Mink the totem in her dreams, running through the woods with the six little mink spirits trailing happily behind.

Sacred Dance and Art

One of the ways I have long made use of animal parts is in sacred totemic dance. I generally dance wearing animal skins, usually a full wolf hide, though I have danced in others as the occasion appears. The animal skins aren't necessary, of course. I wear them as a way to connect with the totems, and also to let the skin spirits "ride" my body during the dance while showing me what it's like to see the world through their eyes for a bit. The same concept can be done with any small bit of bone, fur, or even synthetic representations of the animals and their totems.

Regardless of whether or not you wear any costumery, totemic dance starts with moving like the animal. Don't be alarmed! It's okay if you can't imitate the animal perfectly. After all, human bodies are rather uniquely shaped, resembling little else in the animal kingdom. We have our physical limitations; do your best anyway.

First, study how the animal moves, either in person or on video (YouTube has videos of just about any animal you can think of, from the honey badger to the sea angel to the binturong, and then some). Then try it out for yourself. If you feel self-conscious, practice at home alone; once you feel a little braver, you may try using a full-length mirror to see what your movements look like.

Next, it's time to dance! Contrary to popular belief, you don't necessarily have to dance around an area or even stand upright; it's perfectly possible to dance while sitting or even lying down. What's important is that you're moving to a rhythm, with or without music. Use the animal movements with that rhythm, and invite the totems you're imitating to join you. In fact, they may even have made their presence known while you were practicing, working up to a full dance.

Totemic dance is a fun practice for drum circles and other festival occasions; however, you can also use it for personal ritual use. It's a lovely way to honor the totems, invite them to join you in your celebration, and a great chance to get a sense of what it might be like to be that animal.

Dance isn't the only form of creativity you can use to connect with totems. Any art form can be used to honor them. Ravenari, a very dear friend of mine, has been creating sacred totemic art with a distinctive style for many years. During the artistic process, she connects with a variety of totems that have asked her to make art of them, and the result is some of the most beautiful sacred art I've seen. That connection during the actual creative process is one of the keys to what makes her works so powerful.[24]

In the same way, you can channel totemic energy into your own creativity. You may ask your totems if they wish to have a painting, song, or other creative work made for them, though you may also have them come to you with the request themselves. Some people can settle right into a spiritual mindset when making sacred art, but others prefer a little bit of ritual. You may have a specific set of tools you use, or prepare your space in a particular way. Do whatever you feel you need to do to make the setting right.

What if you don't think you're an artist, but you feel inspired by the works of others? That inspiration can also be a key connection to the totems. I am not much for drawing or painting, but I collect art made by others. I can look at those works and feel the presence of the totems through them, which is why they end up on my altars and other sacred spaces. Choosing a selection of art others have made can be just as creative as making art in the first place.

---

24. You may see Ravenari's work online at http://ravenari.deviantart .com/.

Altars, Sacred Spaces, and Offerings

Earlier I mentioned altars and shrines. One really effective way that a lot of people invite totems into their homes is by maintaining a sacred space for them. This need not be a huge, elaborate room full of altars and devotional art. A portion of a shelf with a few small representations of the totems can be enough. You don't need a bunch of expensive statues and tools, either, though there's nothing wrong with them. Personal artwork, pictures of animals cut out of magazines or printed off the Internet, and even articles or other writing can be just as effective and special.

What's most important is that this place is offered to the totems as their home within your home. They may ask you to do specific things to take care of it, or you may develop rituals of your own. For me, keeping my altars dusted is a ritual in and of itself (and not just due to how fast the dust seems to accumulate!). Whenever I add something new to an altar or include it in a ritual is also a good time to check in with its overall energy to see if it needs any other sort of maintenance or change.

Of course, any space can be sacred. You may not have enough room or privacy in your home for an entire altar setup, but you can still designate a place for the totems; all it takes is intent. Is there a park or other place nearby where you can meditate? Perhaps even a single tree you feel especially connected to? Find a place you can visit to connect with your totems.

It may be tempting to leave offerings at your sacred place, whether in your home or elsewhere, especially food. Food has long been a spiritual offering; food is life, and to offer it is to offer one's own survival. Unfortunately, leaving food where living animals can get to it is very often a bad idea for the animals. Much of what we eat isn't good for other critters and can make them sick or even kill them. Additionally, when wildlife learns to associate humans with food, it frequently goes badly for the wildlife. If they aren't killed outright by being hit by cars or shot by opportunistic hunters, they can make nuisances of themselves, even harming humans with overenthusiastic food-seeking. And over time, if generations of animals become too dependent on humans for food, they can stop passing on the knowledge of how to forage to their young, leaving them vulnerable to starvation if humans cease feeding them.

Volunteer time at shelters and sanctuaries and financial donations to animal-based nonprofits make much better offerings. Additionally, just as we can ask totems for help, they may ask us for help, too. Being able to help may be one of the biggest offerings we can make.

Group Totems

As I mentioned early on in the book, traditionally totems have been associated in many indigenous cultures with groups, such as families or tribes, rather than individuals.

Even if you aren't part of one of these cultures, it is still possible for you to work with a totem as part of a group. There are a few spiritual and magical groups I know personally that have collective totems, and I would imagine they aren't the only ones. Some people research their ancestry and find long-ago-forgotten familial totems that are then revived into modern-day honor.

If you would like to work with a totem as part of a group, the first thing you'll want to do is to identify your group. You might be a part of a spiritual group or organization interested in animal totemism on this level; many newly formed groups seek out spiritual patrons such as deities when they first formally come together, and there's no reason why your group can't also look for guidance and patronage from an animal totem, even if you've been together a while. In fact, you might already have some idea of what the totem of the group is, either through the name of the group (Raventree Coven, Wolf's Howl Shamanic Circle, etc.) or through the totemic experiences of group members, especially if multiple people have worked with the same totem.

On the other hand, your group may be less formal, but no less close, such as a group of good friends. You may all practice various sorts of spirituality but agree that you'd all like to find a totem who will work with the group either together or as individuals. So you all might agree to seek out a group totem, and then work with it on your own terms most of the time, perhaps with periodic group ceremonies and celebrations of the totem. Some groups of friends also end up with informal animal mascots, maybe through a group in-joke or shared experience; the totem of that animal could also potentially be looked to as a possible group protector.

If you know who your ancestral family totem is, you can try contacting them to see if they're still interested in working with you as a member of that family today. Often familial totems are glad to see a renewed interest in them, though some may also have moved on or otherwise no longer protect the family. If you get a positive response from the totem, great! Just be aware that not everyone in your family may be interested in joining you in group totemic work, particularly if they're of a religion that doesn't include (or even discourages) totemism. There may still be family members who are at least curious about what you're doing, even if from a genealogical perspective only.

I've given just a few suggestions of groups that can have totems. Once you have determined your group and everyone is on board as much as they can be, here are some avenues of exploration:

- Check out the family totem angle. Do you know of any animals that may have been totems in your family at one time? Is your last name associated with an animal, such as Wolf, Lamb, or Bird? If your family has any sort of heraldry or similar symbolism from its culture, are there animals on it? Were your ancestors involved in any sort of farming or other animal-related professions? Look at your current family as well; are there any close animal associations there? If there are preexisting totemic connections, are there any traditions associated with them?

· Regardless of who's involved, if your group doesn't yet have a totem, you can do a guided meditation as a group. Have one member read the guided meditation in Appendix B out loud or have it prerecorded so everyone can participate. Before people go into the meditation, make sure they know they are specifically seeking out the group's totem. Once everyone has come back out of the meditation, compare notes and make a list of all the animals that appeared in the meditation. If everyone has a different animal, that's okay. You can then discuss among the group which ones feel especially appropriate, and do more group guided meditations to have everyone go to talk with a specific totem to find out how good a match it is for the group. You may end up with more than one group totem this way; what's important is that the group and the totem(s) agree to work together.

Once your group has determined at least one collective totem, the totem may simply be a sort of group guardian and reminder of your connections to each other. You all may want to have some shared symbol of the totem, such as a small picture or figurine. Some people even get matching tattoos, though this may not be an option for everyone. The totem may also serve as a good rallying point in times of need; if a member of the group passes away, the remaining people may find some solace in the comfort of each other, and use the totem as a reminder that they have that support system even in their loss.

On the other hand, it may take a more active role; here are some possibilities:

- If you are a spiritual or magical group, call the totem to join you at every ritual, festival, and other gathering you do as a group. If there's room, create a temporary or even permanent shrine for the totem where you commonly celebrate.

- If someone in the group is in need and the totem may be able to help, ask for its assistance, if appropriate. For example, if someone is in need of healing and the group totem is Horse, the group may ask Horse to share some of her vitality and strength with the ill person. Or if the group totem cannot help, it may know another who can. Egyptian Crocodile may not be particularly associated with healing, but Egyptian Plover is. Plover's children will routinely remove parasites and old food from the mouths and skin of crocodiles, thereby helping crocodiles stay healthy while the plovers get a meal. Crocodile may be able to facilitate a connection with Plover to bring healing to the sick.

• Traditionally, group totems have often been associated with taboos, certain cultural and behavioral restrictions that are a part of being associated with the totem's group, but which generally benefit the group members in some way. Historically these often included prohibitions against marrying someone with the same totem since they were quite likely to be related to you, or restrictions on eating the flesh of the totem's children. These may not seem so applicable in your case, but ask the totem if it has any taboos or other requirements for the group. They may be as simple as not killing the totem's children, though they may also be more elaborate, such as a protective totem requiring the members of the group to never refuse reasonable amounts of safety and assistance to people and animals in need. It is recommended that before the group formally accepts the totem as their group guardian that the totem should be asked about any taboos or other restrictions.

Tina, Josh, and Erin formed a Wicca-inspired coven when they were in high school. Because they all liked the crows that hung around the schoolyard, they called themselves the Crow Coven. Now that they're a few years older, they only get together when they're all home at holidays. They still want to try to maintain a magical relationship together even when distance separates them, so they ask the totem Crow, who has long been their namesake, to help them maintain that bond. On the evening before they head back to their respective homes, the three friends do a ritual together. They ask Crow to join them as they each make small black cloth pouches with silver feathers painted on the front, and a little lock of hair from each one of them in each of the pouches. Together they say, "Though we may be far away, let these special creations remind us of the strength we have together. Let Crow's strong, swift wings carry our friendship to each other, in good times and in times of need. So mote it be!"

These are just a few ways you can strengthen your connection to the totems, regardless of what model you're working within. As always, take what works best for you, and change or leave the rest.

Conclusion

Animal totemism is a tradition that has existed for thousands of years, and yet as our species has gone through rapid changes in recent centuries, so has the concept of totemism shifted and adapted as well. Although some may feel it is an antiquated practice or a throwback to more "primitive" times, the reality is that there are still many extant cultures that continue to use it even as they and the world around them evolve with the times.

This book is intended to combine the wisdom of these old traditions with the needs and parameters of many people in the twenty-first century—nonindigenous and otherwise. More importantly, it does not turn a blind eye to the realities of the animals themselves. Nobel prize-winning chemist Paul Krutzen has suggested that we are no longer in the Holocene Epoch which began 10,000 years ago, but instead have shifted to the Anthropocene Epoch, marked by the massive effects humanity has had on the planet.

These changes include the mass extinction of numerous species of animals and plants and the increasing threat against countless others. Neither are the other beings of the planet safe; massive machines destroy entire mountains to remove a scant percentage of the coal within, and the rivers are choked with silt. Even the oceans and the rain forests, which together are the respiratory system of the very Earth itself, are increasingly clogged with toxins.

These disasters are the direct result of our disconnection with the world around us; we are so insulated against the processes of life and death we participate in that we have become numb to them. Animal totemism is one way we can rekindle our interest in the world around us and the diversity of beings with whom we share it.

Animal totemism is not just about knowing what your special animal is. I've shown you ways in which the totems can help us to be more aware of the physical environments we are part of…and not just the human-made portions. It is crucial that we make our decisions with these ecosystems and bioregions and their denizens in mind; totemism allows us to make these even more personal. The totems introduce us to their children, and by extension, their homes.

Totemism isn't just about what's around us, however. Our behaviors as individuals and as a species start within. If the well our actions spring from is poisoned, we spread that poison wherever we go. By knowing ourselves more deeply and working to become healthier, more complete human beings, we can spread that greater health throughout a world we have sickened so extensively.

The world we live in is not the world of our ancestors thousands—or even hundreds—of years ago. We face unprecedented problems but also possess unprecedented solutions. We can use our increased connectivity through technology to share solutions, hold accountable perpetrators of environmental and other abuses, and find solace in each other's support. As a result of ongoing civil rights efforts and greater awareness of environmental issues, we are experiencing more social and cultural enlightenment based on compassion and scientific evidence, both of which continue to replace draconian social restrictions and superstitions that excuse harm to other living beings.

There is nothing wrong if all you wish is to receive a bit of guidance from the animal totems in your life. This book can be the beginning of a greater work if you so choose. The Archetypal work helps us to better know ourselves and create more conscious actions; the Bioregional work reminds us of our place in the enormous chorus of nature; and the Correspondences help us bridge the inner and outer with a language we can understand on many levels. Our closest cousins in this world, the animals are guides into these places and levels of being, and they stand to benefit greatly from the work we do.

I will consider it an honor if you use this book to facilitate a path of healing for many, or bring about a positive change in your own life. The tools are there for all of it.

Appendix A:
Animal Nonprofits

One of the best ways you can give back to your totems is to help their physical children, as well as supporting healthy habitats for all. Following is a far-from-complete list of animal- and habitat-based nonprofits I believe are worthy of support. Additionally, check your area for local animal shelters, wildlife refuges and rehab centers, and other small nonprofit organizations that may benefit from your volunteer time or financial donation. There are also a variety of organizations, such as Project Coyote, the Scottish Wildcat Association, and the Cheetah Conservation Fund that are dedicated to one or a few species in particular.

Be aware that different organizations may use funds in their own ways. Some larger groups like to offer gifts like backpacks or stuffed toy animals as incentives for membership and donations. Keep in mind that these cost money, and it's better just to give money without expecting extras in return. You can also find out information about how different organizations use their money and how much goes to actual environmental work (as opposed to operating costs, etc.) at websites like http://www.charitynavigator.org and similar sites.

Defenders of Wildlife
National Headquarters
1130 17th Street, NW
Washington, DC 20036
1-800-385-9712
defenders@mail.defenders.org
http://www.defenders.org
Works to preserve wildlife, particularly large North American predators, as well as their habitat.

World Wildlife Federation (WWF) International
Avenue du Mont Blanc 1196
Gland, Switzerland
+41 22 364 9111
http://www.panda.org

A global organization that has worked for several decades to bring awareness and advocacy regarding endangered species to people worldwide.

The Wilderness Society
1615 M Street NW
Washington, DC 20036
1-800-THE-WILD
http://www.wilderness.org
Many animals that face extinction are vulnerable due to habitat loss; this group works to preserve wilderness areas, to include crucial wildlife habitat.

The Jane Goodall Institute
4245 North Fairfax Drive
Suite 600
Arlington, VA 22203
(703) 682-9220
http://www.janegoodall.org
Using research and educational programs, the Jane Goodall Institute has worked not only to save chimpanzees and their homes, but to bring awareness of habitat and species destruction.

Natural Resources Defense Council
40 West 20th Street
New York, NY 10011
(212) 727-2700
http://www.nrdc.org
Lobbies for the protection of both animals and their
environments, and is also instrumental in helping
communities preserve local habitats.

The Nature Conservancy
4245 North Fairfax Drive, Suite 100
Arlington, VA 22203-1606
(800) 628-6860
http://www.nature.org
Focuses on protecting habitats around the world, and
educating people about the importance of healthy
ecosystems. This includes direct protection of individual
habitats in conjunction with local communities.

The Ocean Conservancy
1300 19th Street, NW
8th Floor
Washington, DC 2003
800-519-1541
http://www.oceanconservancy.org
Works to protect the world's oceans and to create awareness
of how crucial the oceans and their inhabitants are to the
planet's health as a whole.

Animal Welfare Institute
PO Box 3650
Washington, DC 20027
(703) 836-4300
http://www. awionline.org
Since 1951, this organization has worked to protect animals wild and domestic, to include in labs and elsewhere.

The Sierra Club
85 Second Street, 2nd Floor
San Francisco, CA 94105
Phone: 415-977-5500
http://www.sierraclub.org
One of the oldest and largest environmental nonprofits, combines government lobbying with grassroots organization for a variety of ecological causes.

Appendix B:
Guided Meditation
for Finding Totems

Guided meditation is a pretty common practice in Neo-pagan totemism across the board. Just about every book on the subject contains some version of it, and for good reason—it's effective! What it does is get you directly in contact with the totem you're seeking (whether or not you know who it is yet) without the biases of people acting as intermediaries, and without the limitations and suggestions of totem decks. You're opening yourself up to the hidden layers of your psyche and all the totems in the world.

Just to reiterate, guided meditations are not the same as shamanic journeys. A proper journey takes a person deep into the spirit realm, which can be dangerous—there's a reason indigenous shamans have spiritual weapons as well as an array of power animals and other spiritual protectors when they journey. A guided meditation instead takes you to a sort of neutral zone partway between the spirit world and your own psyche, where you and the spirits you meet are on more even footing with each other. This meditation will provide you with a neutral zone where you can continue to meet with totems after you've been introduced.

You can memorize the basic structure of this meditation, have someone read it to you, or even record yourself reading it and play it back. There are no specific times associated with each part of the meditation, so take as long as you need. One thing I have noticed is that people have a tendency to take less time coming out of the meditation than going into it. I would strongly recommend taking at least as much time to come back through the tunnel as you did going into it. This allows you to have ample time to adjust your state of consciousness as you're going into the meditation and coming back to the waking world.

While you are going through the tunnel to find the totem, if you feel the need to end the meditation early, realize that all you need to do to come back to the waking world is to turn around and retrace your steps. If you are already through the tunnel into the place where you can meet the totem and you lose the tunnel, just look down at your feet, and the opening of the tunnel will be right there to take you back home.

Totemic Guided Meditation

Get into a comfortable place and position, and wear something loose and comfortable. Make sure the temperature is right and that you won't be disturbed for the time you need.

Close your eyes, and focus on your breathing. Let the only thing that moves you be the breath going in and out of your body. With each exhalation, let the tension drain from you a little more. With each inhalation, let calm enter your mind. If thoughts arise in your mind, let them drift by like clouds.

When you are ready, visualize a hole in the ground, water, or sky. See it before you, and go to it. Breathe and enter it, going into a tunnel.

Move through the tunnel, whether you walk, run, float, fly, or swim. Move at your own pace.

When you come out of the tunnel, you find yourself in a natural setting where an animal may live. Take some time to explore it. What sort of place are you in? What's there? What's happening?

As you explore, you see an animal coming toward you. How is it behaving? How far away is it?

Let it approach, and greet it. Ask why it, out of all the other animals, appeared. Take some time to talk with each other.

When you are ready to go back, thank the animal for its time, and tell it that this is a place that you can both come to meet with each other again.

Return to the tunnel, and come back home when you're ready. There's no rush; take all the time you need to wake up again.

Further Uses of This Meditation

The version of the meditation above is written for finding a totem for the first time; if you wish to use it to go back and visit that totem again, go to the neutral zone and specifically look for or even call to the totem you seek.

For example, say that when doing the meditation for the very first time, when you were just opening yourself up to the totems and wanted to see who would show up, you ended up being introduced to Coyote. You want to go back and talk to Coyote again. This time, when you go into the meditation, go in with the intent of meeting Coyote, and when you get out of the tunnel, greet him and ask him to join you if he isn't there already.

You can do the same thing if you're looking for other specific totems, even if it's for the first time. Say you want to talk to Blue Jay because you've seen a lot of blue jays around and you want to find out whether that's significant (beyond having a healthy blue jay population in the neighborhood, of course). Just use this meditation for the specific purpose of talking to Blue Jay, and again, if she's not already there when you get through the tunnel, ask her to join you.

Troubleshooting and Tips

- If you're having trouble staying focused and "in" the meditation, like your consciousness keeps fading in and out, you may need to spend more time practicing basic meditation skills. Try meditating only on your breathing, or concentrating on staying as still as possible. You can also meditate while keeping your focus on a specific thought, image, or mantra. Once you feel more able to stay in meditation for long enough to go through this one, give it another try.

- If you try this meditation for the first time and don't find any animals or they all seem distant and don't communicate with you, it doesn't mean you weren't doing it right. It may be that the totem didn't feel ready to come forward or it thought you weren't quite ready to start working with it yet. Give yourself a couple of weeks off and try again. If it takes a while even to see an animal, don't be discouraged; we find our totems when the time is right.

- If you get glimpses of an animal (but nothing clear), or if the animal avoids you, take a break for a couple of weeks, and then go back in and see if the animal shows up again. You can try calling to the animal, though don't be surprised if it still acts shyly. Let it come to you, even if it takes a few meditations. Also, keep in mind that the first animal you see may not be your totem; if other animals happen to show up, pay attention to them as well.

- If you're unsure of what the animal is, do your best to note as many details as possible. Record these as soon as you come out of the meditation, and then go to the Internet or library and start researching animals. You may find the animal exactly as it looked, or very similar, but be sure to verify the animal's identity with it when you go back to visit.

- If the animal is one that scares you or acts aggressively, it doesn't mean it's not your totem. It also isn't automatically your Shadow totem, either; as with any totemic relationship, let the totem reveal its reasons for working with you over time, and do your best to approach the totem as safely as you can. The neutral zone is meant to be safe for all involved. I can tell you that in over a decade of consistent totemic work, a totem has never attempted to harm me in any setting.

- If you just don't feel all that connected to the
  totem that approaches you, give it some time.
  Try talking to the totem about the situation and get
  its perspective. If you still feel it's not "right" for you,
  thank it for its time and consideration, and then
  seek another totem. However, don't be surprised if
  the first totem comes back later on; many times it's
  a matter of us simply not being ready for it yet.

Glossary

Animal Totem: A spiritual being that encompasses all the qualities of a given species of animal, as opposed to an individual animal spirit. For example, the totem Gray Wolf represents all gray wolves instead of an individual gray wolf spirit.

Archetype: The personification or symbolic manifestation of some deep, primal impulse or instinct in the human mind. The Shadow archetype, for example, may represent a certain fear or aggressive urge thought to be socially unacceptable.

Bioregionalism: Identifying a place by naturally occurring physical landmarks, often watersheds, as opposed to human-made landmarks like streets or city limits. Synonymous with ecoregion.

Correspondences: A system or series of concepts, ideas, or things related to each other in a particular pattern; for example, in the Northern Hemisphere, the hottest part of the day is when the sun is in the southern part of the sky. South therefore corresponds to the hottest element, Fire, as well as the middle part of the day.

Cultural Appropriation: The act of taking parts of a particular culture out of their original context and trying to fit them into another culture's context; for example, white people adding bits and pieces of Native American religions to New Age concepts. The general connotation of cultural appropriation is that the people doing the appropriating have more power than the ones being taken from, and the appropriation causes further disempowerment.

Element: In a spiritual or magical sense, this is not related to the scientific periodic table of elements, but rather a more simplified set, the most basic components of matter. The most commonly cited Western elements are earth, air, fire and water (and, more recently, Spirit); also frequently used are the Chinese elements of wood, fire, earth, metal, and water.

Guided Meditation: A form of meditation that has a scripted structure guiding a person through a specific series of images or experiences in the meditation. Some are more freeform, while others follow the script very closely. In totemism, guided meditation is commonly used to help a person meet with totem animals. *See also* Journeying.

Indigenous: Refers to a culture or people who are native to a place, as opposed to more recent immigrants or descendants of immigrants. The actual time a culture must be in a place in order to be considered indigenous is not exact but is generally considered to be measured in thousands of years. Nonindigenous people may arrive in a place where there is already an established indigenous population by various means.

Journeying: In shamanism, journeying is an altered state of consciousness in which the shaman travels to the spirit world to speak with spirits, fight spiritual battles, retrieve lost items or pieces of a client's soul, or explore the spiritual realm, among other purposes. This practice differs from guided meditation in that it takes the person deep into the spirits' territory, whereas guided meditation leads a person into a more neutral zone between physical reality and the spirit realm. *See also* Shamanism.

Neopagan: Literally "new pagan," a term for any of a number of new religious movements and spiritualities dating from the mid-twentieth century and later; these commonly are concerned with reconstructing older pre-Christian religions, or creating new nature-based spiritualities inspired by these old beliefs.

Shamanism: A blanket term for a variety of spiritual, cultural, and practical efforts found in societies worldwide. A shaman is a spiritual specialist who commonly uses ecstatic trance within a cultural framework to act as an intermediary between his or her community and the spirit realm, other communities, other species, etc. The term "shaman" originated with the Evenk of Siberia to describe their particular culture's practitioners but was appropriated by Western anthropologists to apply to similar practitioners in cultures worldwide.

Skin Spirits: A term created by the author to describe the spirits (or spiritual residue/haunts) that remain in an animal's body after death. Skin spirits are not only found in the animal's hide, but also in bones and other remains. While these usually depart as the body decays, preserved remains such as tanned hides may retain their spirits as long as the remains are physically intact.

Social Justice/Social Location: Social justice refers to the goal of creating a society based on equality, justice, and compassion, as well as correcting injustices, discrimination, and bigotry. One's social location refers to such parts of one's identity and being as sex, gender, race, culture, religion, sexuality, (dis)ability, and other health status, etc. Social justice is concerned with achieving equality for all regardless of social location.

Totemism: Traditionally, a system using animals, plants, or other beings and concepts as representatives of groups within a community such as families or clans. Totemism was originally used for group identification as well as determining who could marry whom (usually involving the forbidding of marrying someone with the same totem even if there was no blood relation). The word "totem" is of Ojibwe origin but has been used by anthropologists to refer to similar symbolic systems across a variety of cultures. More recent nonindigenous totemisms have been more individualistic, concerned primarily with self-improvement and reconnecting to the natural world.

Bibliography

Abramms, Bob. "Stuart MacArthur's Universal Corrective Map." 2001. Accessed September 11, 2011. http://www.youtube.com/watch?v=QYuV4eOVz38.

Bonewits, Isaac. "Defining Paganism: Paleo-, Meso-, and Neo-." 2007. Accessed September 11, 2011. http://www.Neopagan.net/PaganDefs.html.

Brown, Joseph Epes. *Animals of the Soul: Sacred Animals of the Oglala Sioux.* Rockport, MA: Element Books, 1997.

Crain, William. *Theories of Development: Concepts and Applications.* 5th ed. Upper Saddle River, NJ: Pearson/Prentice Hall, 2005.

Crowley, Aleister. *777 and Other Qabalistic Writings of Aleister Crowley*. York Beach, ME: Samuel Weiser, 1993.

Dawkins, Richard. *The Greatest Show on Earth: The Evidence for Evolution*. New York: Free Press, 2009.

Duquette, Lon Milo. *The Chicken Qabalah of Rabbi Lamed ben Clifford*. York Beach, ME: Samuel Weiser, 2001.

Endredy, James. *Ecoshamanism: Sacred Practices of Unity, Power & Earth Healing*. Woodbury, MN: Llewellyn Publications, 2005.

Gallegos, Eligio Stephen. *The Personal Totem Pole: Animal Imagery, the Chakras, and Psychotherapy*. Embudo, NM: Moon Bear Press, 1990.

Greer, John Michael. *The Druidry Handbook: Spiritual Practice Rooted in the Living Earth*. York Beach, ME: Weiser Books, 2006.

Hemachandra, Ray A. "Selling the Sacred: American Indians and the New Age." 2003. Accessed September 11, 2011. http://web.williams.edu/anthsoc/native/Selling_the_Sacred.pdf.

Jones, Evan John, and Chas Clifton. *Sacred Mask Sacred Dance*. St. Paul, MN: Llewellyn Publications, 1997.

Jung, Carl. *Man and His Symbols*. Garden City, NY: Doubleday and Company, 1964.

———. *The Archetypes and the Collective Unconscious*. Princeton, NJ: Princeton University Press, 1981.

Laurie, Erynn Rowan. *Ogam: Weaving Word Wisdom*. Stafford, UK: Megalithica Books, 2007.

Levi-Strauss, Claude. *Totemism*. Boston: Beacon Press, 1971.

Lopez, Barry Holstun. *Of Wolves and Men*. New York: Scribner, 1979.

Macy, Joanna, and Molly Young Brown. *Coming Back to Life: Practices to Reconnect Our Lives, Our World*. Gabriola Island: New Society Publishers, 1998.

Mitchell, Stephen A. and Margaret J. Black. *Freud and Beyond: A History of Modern Psychoanalytic Thought*. New York: Basic Books, 1995.

Morris, Brian. *The Power of Animals: An Ethnography*. Oxford: Berg, 1998.

Plotkin, Bill. *Nature and the Human Soul: Cultivating Wholeness and Community in a Fragmented World*. Novato, CA: New World Library, 2008.

Ravenari. "Wolf: Teacher Give-away." n.d. Accessed September 11, 2011. http://www.wildspeak.com/totems /wolf.html.

Saunders, Nicholas J. *Living Wisdom: Animal Spirits*. Boston: Little, Brown and Company, 1995.

Starhawk. *The Earth Path: Grounding Your Spirit in the Rhythms of Nature*. San Francisco: HarperSanFrancisco, 2005.

Whitcomb, Bill. *The Magician's Companion: A Practical and Encyclopedic Guide to Magical and Religious Symbolism*. St. Paul, MN: Llewellyn Publications, 2002.

Recommended Reading

Andrews, Ted. *Animal-Speak: The Spiritual and Magical Powers of Creatures Great and Small.* St. Paul, MN: Llewellyn Publications, 1996.

———. *Animal-Wise: The Spirit Language and Signs of Nature.* Jackson, TN: Dragonhawk Publishing, 1999.

Bennett, Hal Zina. *Spirit Animals and the Wheel of Life: Earth-Centered Practices for Daily Living.* Newburyport, MA: Hampton Roads Publishing, 2000.

Brinkerhoff, Marc. *Your Spirit Animal Helpers: The Divine Guardians of Your Happiness.* New York: International Rights, 1997.

Green, Susie. *Animal Messages*. London: Cico Books, 2005.

Hausman, Gerald. *Meditations With Animals*. Rochester, VT: Bear and Company, 1986.

Lopez, Barry Holstun. *Of Wolves and Men*. New York: Scribner, 1978.

Roderick, Timothy. *The Once Unknown Familiar*. St. Paul, MN: Llewellyn Publications, 1994.

Shepard, Paul, and Barry Sanders. *The Sacred Paw: The Bear in Nature, Myth, and Literature*. New York: Arkana Books, 1985.

Index

GET MORE AT **LLEWELLYN.COM**

Visit us online to browse hundreds of our books and decks, plus sign up to receive our e-newsletters and exclusive online offers.

- **Free tarot readings • Spell-a-Day • Moon phases**
- **Recipes, spells, and tips • Blogs • Encyclopedia**
- **Author interviews, articles, and upcoming events**

GET SOCIAL WITH **LLEWELLYN**

Find us on Facebook
www.Facebook.com/LlewellynBooks

Follow us on
twitter™
www.Twitter.com/Llewellynbooks

GET BOOKS AT **LLEWELLYN**

LLEWELLYN ORDERING INFORMATION

Order online: Visit our website at www.llewellyn.com to select your books and place an order on our secure server.

Order by phone:
- Call toll free within the U.S. at 1-877-NEW-WRLD (1-877-639-9753)
- Call toll free within Canada at 1-866-NEW-WRLD (1-866-639-9753)
- We accept VISA, MasterCard, and American Express

Order by mail:
Send the full price of your order (MN residents add 6.875% sales tax) in U.S. funds, plus postage and handling to: Llewellyn Worldwide, 2143 Wooddale Drive Woodbury, MN 55125-2989

POSTAGE AND HANDLING:
STANDARD: (U.S. & Canada)
(Please allow 12 business days)
$25.00 and under, add $4.00.
$25.01 and over, FREE SHIPPING.

INTERNATIONAL ORDERS (airmail only):
$16.00 for one book, plus $3.00 for each additional book.

Visit us online for more shipping options.
Prices subject to change.

FREE CATALOG!

To order, call
1-877-
NEW-WRLD
ext. 8236
or visit our
website

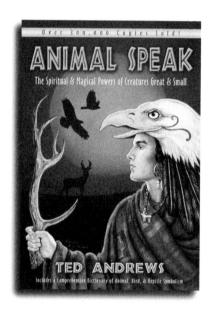

ANIMAL SPEAK

The Spiritual & Magical Powers of Creatures Great & Small

TED ANDREWS

Includes a Comprehensive Dictionary of Animal, Bird, & Reptile Symbolism

Animal-Speak
The Spiritual & Magical Powers
of Creatures Great and Small
TED ANDREWS

The animal world has much to teach us. Some animals are experts at survival and adaptation, some never get cancer, and some embody strength and courage, while others exude playfulness. Animals remind us of the potential we can unfold, but before we can learn from them, we must first be able to speak with them.

In this book, myth and fact are combined in a manner that will teach you how to speak and understand the language of the animals in your life. *Animal-Speak* helps you meet and work with animals as totems and spirits—by learning the language of their behaviors within the physical world. It provides techniques for reading signs and omens in nature so you can open yourself to higher perceptions and even prophecy. It reveals the hidden, mythical, and realistic roles of 45 animals, 60 birds, 8 insects, and 6 reptiles.

Animals will become a part of you, revealing to you the majesty and divine in all life. They will restore your childlike wonder of the world and strengthen your belief in magic, dreams, and possibilities.

978-0-87542-028-8, 400 pp., 7 x 10   **$21.95**

ANIMAL MAGICK

D.J. CONWAY

The Art of Recognizing & Working with Familiars

Animal Magick
The Art of Recognizing & Working with Familiars
D. J. CONWAY

The use of animal familiars began long before the Middle Ages in Europe. It can be traced to ancient Egypt and beyond. To most people, a familiar is a witch's companion, a small animal that helps the witch perform magick, but you don't have to be a witch to have a familiar. In fact, you don't even have to believe in familiars to have one. You may already have a physical familiar living in your home in the guise of a pet. Or you may have an astral-bodied familiar if you are intensely drawn to a particular creature that is impossible to have in the physical. There are definite advantages to befriending a familiar. They make excellent companions, even if they are astral creatures. If you work magick, the familiar can aid by augmenting your power. Familiars can warn you of danger, and they are good healers.

Most books on animal magick are written from the viewpoint of the Native American. This book takes you into the exciting field of animal familiars from the European Pagan viewpoint. It gives practical meditations, rituals, and power chants for enticing, befriending, understanding, and using the magick of familiars.

978-1-56718-168-5, 288 pp., 6 x 9   **$15.95**

ANIMAL OMENS

Victoria Hunt

Animal Omens
Victoria Hunt

As fellow creatures who are uniquely attuned to the earth's
energies, animals provide us with hidden messages every
day—we just need to learn how to read them.

This personal and engaging book shows you how each
animal carries a particular omen—a personal and significant message—helping to guide you on your life path.
Twenty-nine true animal encounter stories are followed
by insightful explanations of each animal's corresponding
omen, and how their messages can help you make important life decisions. Not sure whether it's the right time to
switch jobs or relocate? An unexpected visit from a linger-
ing butterfly can signal a period of imminent change and
transformation in your life.

Organized alphabetically by animal and compact
enough to carry, this inspirational reference guide can be
taken along on introspective nature walks. Foster a closer
connection with nature and learn about yourself—with a
little bit of animal wisdom.

978-0-7387-1377-9, 192 pp., 5 x 7   **$15.95**

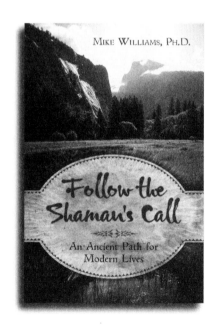

MIKE WILLIAMS, PH.D.

Follow the Shaman's Call

An Ancient Path for
Modern Lives

Follow the Shaman's Call
An Ancient Path for Modern Lives
MIKE WILLIAMS

Drawing on 30,000 years of primeval wisdom, this engaging, hands-on guide teaches you how to transform your increasingly busy and stressful life by following the ancient shamanic path of your ancestors. You'll discover how to meet your spirit guides, journey to the otherworlds for healing and self-empowerment, and bring back lost souls.

As you begin to understand the powerful hidden forces of the unseen world, you'll also learn how to apply the knowledge in a variety of practical ways: predicting the future and understanding the past, using dreamwork to find answers to problems, and clearing your house of negativity and stale influences.

Written to appeal to both beginning and experienced practitioners, *Follow the Shaman's Call* shows how to use shamanic practices to take charge of your life, heal your friends and community, and live in harmony with the world.

978-0-7387-1984-9, 264 pp., 6 x 9   **$16.95**

The Healing Wisdom of Birds
An Everyday Guide to Their
Spiritual Songs & Symbolism
LESLEY MORRISON

As spiritual guides, otherworldly allies, and magical companions, birds have been revered for milennia. This comprehensive collection of bird spirituality explores the rich beliefs and practices surrounding the winged ones—and how these venerated creatures can guide us today.

Drawing on mythology and traditions of worldwide shamanic cultures—from modern times to the Bronze Age—Lesley Morrison examines avian spirituality from all angles: what birds have symbolized through the ages and why; bird deities from Aphrodite to the Hindu goddess Saraswati; their presence in ancient cave art, shapeshifting rituals, magic practices, and religion; and the unique relationship birds share with shamans and other magical people.

From the five stages of soul alchemy to find-ing your bird totem, The Healing Wisdom of Birds offers practical ways to connect with these sacred creatures.

978-0-7387-1882-8, 240 pp., 5³⁄₁₆ x 8 $15.95

To order, call 1-877-NEW-WRLD
Prices subject to change without notice
Order at Llewellyn.com 24 hours a day, 7 days a week!

Shamanism

For Beginners

Walking with the World's Healers
of Earth and Sky

JAMES ENDREDY

Shamanism for Beginners
Walking With the World's Healers of Earth and Sky
James Endredy

Interest in shamanism is on the rise, and people are eager to integrate this intriguing tradition into their own lives. *Shamanism for Beginners* introduces the spiritual beliefs and customs of the shaman—a spiritual leader, visionary, healer, diviner, walker between worlds, and so much more.

How is one called to be a shaman? How is a shaman initiated? Where does a shaman's power come from? Exploring the practices and beliefs of tribes around the world, James Endredy sheds light on the entire shamanic experience. The fascinating origins and evolution of shamanism are examined, along with power places, tools (costume, drum, sweat lodge, medicine wheel), sacred plants, and the relationship between the shaman and spirits. Enriched with the author's personal stories and quotes from actual shaman elders and scholars, Endredy concludes with incredible feats of shamans, healing techniques, and ruminations on the future of this remarkable tradition.

978-0-7387-1562-9, 288 pp., 5³⁄₁₆ x 8   **$14.95**